Toward Competition
in
Local Telephony

AEI STUDIES IN TELECOMMUNICATIONS DEREGULATION
J. Gregory Sidak and Paul W. MacAvoy, series editors

TOWARD COMPETITION IN LOCAL TELEPHONY
William J. Baumol and J. Gregory Sidak

Toward Competition
in
Local Telephony

William J. Baumol
J. Gregory Sidak

THE MIT PRESS
Cambridge, Massachusetts
London, England

and

THE AMERICAN ENTERPRISE INSTITUTE
FOR PUBLIC POLICY RESEARCH
Washington, D.C.

Published by

The MIT Press
Cambridge, Massachusetts
London, England

and

The American Enterprise Institute for Public Policy Research
Washington, D.C.

Library of Congress Cataloging-in-Publication Data

Baumol, William J.
    Toward competition in local telephony / William J. Baumol, J.
Gregory Sidak.
        p.   cm. — (AEI studies in telecommunications deregulation)
    Includes bibliographical references and indexes.
    ISBN 0-262-02369-5
    1. Telephone—United States—Deregulation. 2. Telephone
    companies—United States. I. Sidak, J. Gregory. II. Title.
III. Series.
HE8819.b38 1994
384.6'3—dc20   93-28956
                                                CIP

Printed in the United States of America

Contents

Foreword

DRAMATIC ADVANCES IN COMMUNICATIONS and information technologies are imposing severe strains on a government regulatory apparatus devised in the pioneer days of radio and are raising policy questions with large implications for American economic performance and social welfare. Is federal telecommunications regulation impeding competition and innovation, and has this indeed become its principal if unstated function? Is regulation inhibiting the dissemination of ideas and information through electronic media? Does the licensing regime for the electromagnetic spectrum allocate that resource to its most productive uses? If telecommunications regulation is producing any of these ill effects, what are the costs and offsetting benefits and what should be done?

William J. Baumol and J. Gregory Sidak's study of economic principles for managing the transition from regulation to competition in local telephone service is one of a series of research monographs addressing these questions commissioned by the American Enterprise Institute's Telecommunications Deregulation Project. The AEI project is intended to produce new empirical research on the entire range of telecommunications policy issues, with particular emphasis on identifying reforms to federal and state regulatory policies that will advance rather than inhibit innovation and consumer welfare. We hope this research will be useful to legislators and public officials at all levels of government, and to the business executives and, most of all, the consumers who must live with their policies. The monographs have been written and edited to be accessible to readers with no specialized knowledge of communications technologies or economics; we hope they will find a place in courses on regulated industries and communications policy in economics and communications departments and in business, law, and public policy schools.

Each monograph in the Telecommunications Deregulation Project has been discussed and criticized in draft form at an AEI seminar involving federal and state regulators, jurists, business executives, professionals, and academic experts with a wide range of interests and viewpoints, and has been reviewed and favorably reported by two anonymous academic referees selected by the MIT Press. I wish to thank all of them for their contributions, noting, however, that the final exposition and conclusions are entirely the responsibility of the author of each monograph.

I am particularly grateful to Dean Paul W. MacAvoy of the Yale School of Management and J. Gregory Sidak, resident scholar at AEI, for conceiving and overseeing the project's research and seminars, and to Frank Urbanowski, Terry Vaughn, and Ann Sochi of the MIT Press, for their support and steady counsel in seeing the research through to publication.

CHRISTOPHER C. DEMUTH
President, American Enterprise Institute
for Public Policy Research

Acknowledgments

MANY, IF NOT MOST, of the ideas in this monograph can be traced to a collaboration over many years between one of us (WJB) and Robert D. Willig. The magnitude of our debt to him is inestimable. We are also extremely grateful to Barbara Cherry, Frank J. Gumper, John R. Haring, Jerry Hausman, Charles L. Jackson, Stephen B. Levinson, Robert E. Lloyd, Bill Loughrey, Edward D. Lowry, Paul W. MacAvoy, Andrew J. Margeson, Elliott E. Maxwell, John W. Mayo, Gail Garfield Schwartz, William Shew, John Vickers, Stephen F. Williams, John C. Wohlstetter, and anonymous referees selected by the MIT Press for their careful reading of the manuscript and their valuable suggestions. We have also benefited from the useful suggestions of participants in a roundtable discussion of a draft of the study at the American Enterprise Institute in March 1993. Each of the commenters acknowledged above has expressed some disagreement or reservations about various points in the monograph, and we regret that it is not possible to satisfy them all, though we have amended many passages in accord with their suggestions. Finally, we wish to thank Patricia McCloskey, who prepared the manuscript for publication, with assistance from Douglas Ashton and David Friedman.

WILLIAM J. BAUMOL
J. GREGORY SIDAK

About the Authors

WILLIAM J. BAUMOL is Director of the C.V. Starr Center for Applied Economics at New York University and Professor Emeritus at Princeton University, where he held the Joseph Douglas Green 1895 Chair in economics. During a career spanning more than forty-five years, he has made significant contributions in almost every field of economics. He has published more than 400 articles in professional journals and is the author or coauthor of more than two dozen books, including *Entrepreneurship, Management, and the Structure of Payoffs* (1993), *Economics: Principles and Policy* (5th ed. 1991), *Contestable Markets and the Theory of Industry Structure* (rev. ed. 1988), *The Theory of Environmental Policy* (2d ed. 1988), and *Superfairness* (1986).

Dr. Baumol's work on contestable markets caused a fundamental reexamination of how natural monopolies should be regulated. He has testified in numerous regulatory proceedings and antitrust cases and has been a frequent consultant to AT&T since the 1960s. The Interstate Commerce Commission relied heavily upon his scholarship in its deregulation of railroad rates in the 1980s.

Dr. Baumol is a past president of the American Economic Association, the recipient of numerous professional awards, and a member of the National Academy of Sciences. He received his B.S.S. from the College of the City of New York in 1942 and his Ph.D. from the University of London in 1949.

J. GREGORY SIDAK is a Resident Scholar at the American Enterprise Institute for Public Policy Research, where he directs the Telecommunications Deregulation Project. He is also Senior Lecturer at the Yale School of Management, and Counsel to the law firm of King & Spalding.

As an attorney in government and in private practice, Mr. Sidak has worked on antitrust and regulatory matters concerning the telecommunications industry. He served as Deputy General Counsel of the Federal Communications Commission from 1987 to 1989, and as Senior Counsel and Economist to the Council of Economic Advisers in the Executive Office of the President from 1986 to 1987. He has published articles on antitrust law, telecommunications regulation, corporate governance, and constitutional law in numerous scholarly journals.

Mr. Sidak received A.B. (1977) and A.M. (1981) degrees in economics and a J.D. (1981) from Stanford University. From 1981 to 1982, he was a law clerk to Judge Richard A. Posner of the United States Court of Appeals for the Seventh Circuit.

Toward Competition
in
Local Telephony

1

Introduction

> Eventually, U.S. households will have hundreds or even thousands of television programs available to them on demand . . . . Local telephone monopolies will fall victim to ubiquitous pocket telephones that connect through the spectrum. Dial-up electronic advertising will make it possible to find a job opening or a used car without even picking up a newspaper. The losers in this battle will perhaps have the "satisfaction" that they delayed progress for a while—at the public's expense.
>
> —*Robert W. Crandall*[1]

THE MOST NOTABLE FEATURE of the Modification of Final Judgment (MFJ) that ended in 1982 the Justice Department's prosecution against the American Telephone and Telegraph Company was its divorce of the local telephone companies—the Baby Bells—from their parent company.[2] The firms that operate in the local arena, generically called the local exchange carriers (LECs), consist predominantly of the regional Bell operating companies (RBOCs) that occupy about 80 percent of this segment of the industry. Firms such as GTE and Sprint (the latter of which includes the former Centel and United Telecom)

---

1. Robert W. Crandall, *Regulating Communications: Creating Monopoly While "Protecting" Us From It,* BROOKINGS REV., vol. 10, no.3, at 29 (Summer 1992).

2. United States v. American Tel. & Tel. Co., 552 F. Supp. 131 (D.D.C. 1982), *aff'd sub nom.*, Maryland v. United States, 460 U.S. 1001 (1983). For an exhaustive analysis of the MFJ and its subsequent interpretation, see MICHAEL K. KELLOGG, JOHN THORNE & PETER W. HUBER, FEDERAL TELECOMMUNICATIONS LAW (Little, Brown & Co. 1992).

also are classed as LECs, though they are less regulated than the RBOCs.

The Motivation for Divorcing the Local Exchange Carriers

The RBOCs were separated from AT&T because it was believed that they possessed bottleneck facilities that no other carrier could profitably supply—facilities that consequently conferred monopoly power upon the RBOCs. Those who designed the MFJ believed that, without such a separation of the companies, AT&T could not be left free to embark on new enterprises made possible by rapid technical progress in computation and telecommunications. It was believed that continued possession of the local exchange facilities would enable AT&T to obtain monopoly power in these new fields as well, even if such monopoly power were "unnatural," because it offered no cost advantage over multifirm operation.

These concerns, together with the desire for gradual or even immediate deregulation of the interexchange (long-distance) services, seemed to dictate separation of AT&T from the LECs. AT&T was presumably to be granted the benefits of deregulation with all deliberate speed, though the execution of this program has proved, predictably, to be exceedingly slow. But the local carriers, with their putative monopoly power, were to continue to be regulated closely for the foreseeable future, lest they use that power to exploit their customers or to undermine competition in closely related fields of endeavor.

The Evolution of Competition Since the Modification of Final Judgment

Since the adoption of the MFJ, both the pertinent facts and the climate of opinion have changed considerably. Changes in market structure and technology have made less clear the benefits and costs of extensive regulation of local telephone service. Moreover, despite the largely unmerited unpopularity of the freeing of air passenger service from economic regulation, recognition of the heavy social costs of governmental intrusion into pricing, investment, and other such business decisions has continued to grow.[3] The result has been a gradual but

3. The benefits to consumers from airline deregulation are surveyed in 1988

steady erosion of the constraints upon the operations of the LECs. More than that, the growing awareness of the costs of regulation has prompted a reexamination of the logical basis for those restraints, as well as a search for an alternative arrangement in which competition, partial deregulation, and continued full regulation would each be assigned an appropriate place, one consistent with promotion of the general welfare. The legislatures and public utilities commissions of a number of states, notably Illinois and California, participated in the process, revising laws and reviewing regulatory principles in extensive hearings.[4] Economic analysis has played a surprisingly substantial role in this review.

Our purpose is to gather together the strands of that economic analysis—which has been remarkably consistent, even when the economist witnesses have represented opposing parties in regulatory or judicial proceedings. Excepting some dispute over details, the materials that follow undertake to provide a consensus of the views of the economists directly concerned with the issues. By design, we focus on the relevant economic principles for deregulation and residual regulation of local telephony. We do not attempt to provide either an empirical estimate of the state of competition in the local exchange market at a given moment or the extended implications of any single court ruling or regulatory proceeding at the state or federal level. These latter topics will be addressed by others in subsequent monographs in the American Enterprise Institute's series on telecommunications deregulation.

Subjects to Be Examined

We examine a variety of interrelated subjects that together constitute a program for deregulating the local telephone companies, to the extent that market conditions and the public interest require it. We explain the logic of such a program and discuss, in particular,

---

ECONOMIC REPORT OF THE PRESIDENT 199–229. *See also* STEVEN A. MORRISON & CLIFFORD WINSTON, THE EVOLUTION OF THE AIRLINE INDUSTRY (Brookings Institution, forthcoming 1994).

4. Alternative Regulatory Frameworks for Local Exchange Carriers, Dkt. No. I.87-11-033, 33 C.P.U.C.2d 43, 107 P.U.R.4th 1 (1989); Illinois Bell Tel. Co.: Proposed Restructuring & Increase in Rates, 108 P.U.R.4th 89 (1989).

- the developments that may call for partial deregulation, enhanced flexibility in regulation, or both

- the appropriate criteria for judging whether and to what extent it is desirable to free portions of local telephone service from regulation entirely, or to increase the flexibility of their regulation

- the rules that should govern the choice of which local services, if any, to deregulate completely, which to deregulate in part, and which to continue under full regulation

- the rules that should constrain the decisions of local telephone companies in their production of services that continue to be regulated, partially or comprehensively

- the rules that should govern the pricing of final products

- the rules that should govern the pricing of manufactured inputs, or intermediate goods

- the practical role of Ramsey pricing in the regulation of local telecommunications services

- the public interest in the line-of-business restrictions on the RBOCs and in restraints on competition between local telephone companies and suppliers of cable television.

The text of this monograph is intended to be accessible to non-economists and therefore assumes no special technical knowledge. We use footnotes, and in one case a mathematical appendix, to direct the reader to the original literature in scholarly journals or to present more rigorous demonstrations of the propositions under discussion.

An Outline of the Conclusions

Our least surprising conclusion is that, wherever they can be relied upon to do the job, market forces are preferable to governmental intervention. Whenever competition has become sufficiently powerful to protect the legitimate interests of both consumers and related firms, the local telephone company should be granted full freedom from regulation, subject only to surveillance by the regulatory agency to confirm that market forces are operating as expected and have not eroded.

Much more surprising is our conclusion that economic analysis has already laid out exhaustively and definitively the optimal regulatory regime for those services not suitable for complete deregulation. This analysis proceeds on the premise—almost universally accepted in principle, although widely violated in practice—that the proper role of regulation is that of a substitute for competitive market forces where those forces are weak or absent. The regulator's task then becomes a two-part undertaking: first, to determine the rules of behavior that the regulated firm could have been expected to follow if it had operated free of regulation in a market with fully effective competitive forces; second, to constrain the regulated firm to behave as it would in such a competitive market, and to circumscribe its behavior *no less and no more than this*.

From its investigations of the behavior of competitive firms, economic analysis has derived the information necessary to execute the first of these tasks: Economic theory provides an extensive description of the pricing, investment, and other decisions that the firm would make in a fully competitive market. This descriptive material provides the guidelines for regulation dedicated to eliciting competitive behavior from the regulated firm. There is a complication, however. "Fully effective competition," in the sense appropriate here, is not the perfect competition that underlies neoclassical microeconomics. Economies of scale and scope apparently pervade at least portions of some telecommunications services, and so perfect competition is an inappropriate standard for regulation in this arena. The marginal-cost pricing that prevails under perfect competition would condemn the firm with scale economies to insolvency; this very fact demonstrates conclusively that some other form of competition must serve as the proper standard for firm behavior for our purposes. In any event, it seems improbable that telecommunications services can ever be provided, as perfect competition requires, by myriad firms all of negligible size.

All this drives the analyst to seek another competitive standard as the model for regulation. Such a theoretical standard—*perfect contestability*—is available. Here, we will set out the portions of the theory of perfect contestability required for our discussion, and show what regulatory rules emerge from the structure of this competitive form.

But that digression in no way undermines the conclusion that the regulatory principles and rules required to promote the public interest are known and understood. The following pages describe these rules and explain their logic and implications.

As to the current state of competition facing the local exchange carriers, the conclusion is mixed. The local telephone companies increasingly find themselves in competitive arenas, partly as a result of their own move into services previously offered only by firms specializing in long-distance communication. In addition, there has been some entry by new firms, and the prospect of still more entry, into the local activities that are the primary source of concern about the possession of monopoly power. Entry into these local activities has largely taken the form of radio-based services, such as cellular telephony, and local fiber networks (sometimes called metropolitan-area networks, or MANs). More competition is on the horizon, but so far its arrival has been handicapped by a combination of regulatory impediments and the slow adoption of several facilitating provisions. These include the unbundling of services and the selection of defensible access prices, which protect entrants from cross-subsidies and high interconnection prices that can threaten new competitors' survival and growth.

The public interest will be promoted by freedom of entry into the local telephone services and related arenas. In some of these areas—the natural monopoly arenas of local telecommunications—entry probably will not occur even under the best of circumstances, or, if it does take place, it will not last, at least under current technology. But in other areas, competition may flourish. Given the acceptance of the rules to be described here as instruments to prevent cross-subsidy, predatory pricing, and competition-stifling price discrimination in the sale of inputs to competitors, and given the requirement that full interconnection be provided on equal terms to all qualified applicants, the market will be able to determine which activities in the local arena are truly natural monopolies and which are "naturally competitive." With the local markets organized in this way, entry will occur only where it best serves the public interest, and entrants will be able to survive in good health. In the areas of natural monopoly the rules are designed to approximate the results that characterize a competitive market, and therefore it can be hoped that they will serve the public interest nearly as well as a competitive market can.

2

Actual and Prospective
Competition in Local Telephony

WITHOUT QUESTION, substantial competition pervades some activities of the local telephone companies. In other portions of their operations, however, competition is weak or virtually nonexistent, although manifestations on the horizon suggest that it may not be absent for long. But it is probably undesirable for even the competitive portions of the operations of the local exchange carriers (LECs) simply to be left to fend for themselves, for the LECs' monopoly services constitute inputs for the activities of the rivals of these firms in other arenas—inputs without which the rivals cannot hope to operate. These monopoly services, consequently, are deemed "bottlenecks" or "essential facilities"—meaning that a LEC, if it were to operate completely without regulatory constraint, could use the services or facilities in question to force rivals to bend to its will or to destroy those rivals altogether. This is the fundamental complicating phenomenon that besets the deregulation of local telephone service. Competition in the local arena is provided or threatened from a bewildering array of sources: the interexchange carriers (IXCs), overlapping LECs, resellers, cable television firms, private bypass arrangements, cellular telephone and other wireless services, and local fiber-optic networks. This is the cast of characters in the current chapter.

Competition Between the LECs and the Interexchange Carriers

Let us examine briefly how competition has evolved in local telecommunications. Soon after the Modification of Final Judgment, it was recognized that there would be some competition between the LECs and the interexchange carriers such as AT&T, MCI, and Sprint. Yet the extent to which competition between these two groups has grown was not widely foreseen.[1] The primary arena in which that competition has occurred is the transmission of messages within local areas (the local access and transport areas, or LATAs). Intrastate telecommunications service does not fall under the direct jurisdiction of the Federal Communications Commission, and it soon became clear that state regulatory agencies would not prevent the LECs from providing long-distance services within the boundaries of an individual LATA. With both LECs and IXCs able to participate in the lucrative intraLATA intrastate market, firms in both these groups could be expected to pursue business in this arena with vigor. That is precisely what has occurred.

The growth of competition here posed a disturbing dilemma, however. The LECs argued that full regulation as monopoly suppliers made it impossible for them to compete effectively. That is not to say that the IXCs were left free to compete without constraint. AT&T, in particular, continued to find itself constrained by regulatory intervention both by the FCC at the federal level and by the public utilities commissions of the individual states. Nevertheless, in intrastate services, the LECs claimed that deregulation of their activities was trailing that of AT&T, presumably because the LECs were the residual proprietors of all the substantive bottleneck services.

---

1. For an illuminating contemporary analysis of AT&T's possible strategic objectives in settling the divestiture suit and consenting to the MFJ, see Paul W. MacAvoy & Kenneth Robinson, *Winning by Losing: The AT&T Settlement and Its Impact on Telecommunications*, 1 YALE J. ON REG. 1 (1983).

The LECs' Bottleneck Services

The LECs do continue to possess bottleneck services, even though competition threatens to erode or even to eliminate them. This constitutes legitimate grounds to continue regulating the LECs. The primary bottleneck is constituted by the facilities used to supply access service—that is, the service that provides the connection between messages received from outside areas and the local loop to which a particular subscriber is attached. For local service, at least until recently, it generally has been deemed wasteful to include two or more rival suppliers, since that would entail duplication of facilities (the wires leading into the individual residence or business location). Moreover, it was judged that in this field a multiplicity of suppliers could not long survive, given the cost that their presence imposes and the probable inconvenience to subscribers. As a result, operation of the local loop and the provision of access to it were considered to constitute a natural monopoly from which no substantial deviation was possible.[2] The switches and other equipment used in providing access then were considered to be a bottleneck facility, because no interexchange carrier could deliver a message to the intended recipient's telephone through the local loop without purchasing the access service from the local exchange carrier.

That this transaction constitutes sale of a service by a monopolist to a set of purchasers who compete with one another was complication enough. This state of affairs calls for the usual restraints upon the monopoly seller to ensure that it does not exploit its customers. The situation was rendered even more complex by the competition between the LECs and the IXCs for intraLATA service to subscribers. For the LEC now supplies an essential service—access to the local loop—both

---

2. Some have argued that a market structure of overlapping local exchange carriers, which existed in many American cities until roughly 1915, could or would have survived if interconnection between competing LECs had been required, if AT&T had been prevented from acquiring competitors, and if exclusive franchises had not become politically expedient. *See* MICHAEL K. KELLOGG, JOHN THORNE & PETER W. HUBER, FEDERAL TELECOMMUNICATIONS LAW 12–17 (Little, Brown & Co. 1992). For an analysis of the effect of political constraints on this early market structure, see William P. Barnett & Glenn R. Carroll, *How Institutional Constraints Affected the Organization of Early U.S. Telephony*, 9 J. LAW, ECON. & ORG. 98 (1993).

to itself and to its rivals in the market for intraLATA service. As a consequence, a LEC unconstrained by regulation is in a position not only to favor one IXC over another but, more important, to supply access to itself on terms that favor its own competitive position in the intraLATA markets. The solution to this problem, to which considerable attention will be devoted later in this monograph, requires carefully designed rules on the pricing of intermediate inputs such as access, at least until effective competition in access services has become established.

Prospective Sources of Competition in the Supply of Access

The nature of the access-pricing issue is not our primary concern at this point. Rather, the subject of this chapter is the current state of competition in the markets at issue, and the prospects for competition in these markets in the future.[3] Access, as we have seen, is a service in which substantial and effective competition was believed to be unlikely. This view is no longer strongly or universally held. As we will see now, competition may arise, or already exists, on several different fronts.

Customer Bypass. From the beginning it was recognized that access service was unlikely to be immune from competition. In particular, large customers such as the Department of Defense or the television networks could bypass the facilities of the local exchange carrier by constructing lines that fed directly from the switches of the interexchange carrier into the internal switchboard (the private branch exchange, or PBX) of the large subscriber.[4] Where the subscriber's volume of telecommunications business is sufficient, this sort of bypass

---

3. A forthcoming monograph in the American Enterprise Institute series on telecommunications deregulation, by Bridger M. Mitchell and Ingo Vogelsang, will address the subject of this chapter with greater empirical detail than space permits us to undertake here. For a provocative assessment asserting that substantial competition is imminent in the local loop—but absent in the interexchange market—see PETER W. HUBER, MICHAEL K. KELLOGG & JOHN THORNE, THE GEODESIC NETWORK II: 1993 REPORT ON COMPETITION IN THE TELEPHONE INDUSTRY (The Geodesic Co. 1992).

4. *See* BRIDGER M. MITCHELL & INGO VOGELSANG, TELECOMMUNICATIONS PRICING: THEORY AND PRACTICE 131–34 (Cambridge Univ. Press 1991).

may actually constitute the more efficient arrangement. "Uneconomic bypass," however, was also threatened as a possible consequence of any overpricing of access service by the LEC. If a LEC were to use its monopoly position to overcharge its customers, it could expect the punishment to fit the crime if those customers were sufficiently large and powerful. Where bypass actually used greater quantities of resources than LEC-supplied access but the price charged by the LEC exceeded the cost of such inefficient bypass sufficiently, the subscriber would find the less efficient arrangement nevertheless to be the more profitable.

Uneconomic bypass may also have resulted from regulatory intervention. Regulators have been known to enforce high access charges as a source of revenues for cross-subsidies to residential customers. Often LECs are not allowed to lower their prices to their larger customers in areas densely populated by them, where access competition is highest, even if the incremental cost of such service is low. Here, any loss in economic efficiency is clearly attributable to the actions of regulators. Early in the game, then, both efficient and inefficient bypass became a source of competition in the sale of access services—but only for a limited class of customers. The price of access to those large customers for telecommunications services was forced down to economic levels by market pressures rather than regulatory intervention.

Resale. These new forms of competitive services have been available largely to business or governmental customers, and primarily to such customers who purchase telecommunications services in substantial volume. Nevertheless, the competitiveness that is thereby injected does encompass a considerable portion of the market, if measured in terms of revenues received rather than sheer number of customers. It is an industry rule of thumb that local exchange carriers obtain 80 percent of their total revenues from 20 percent of their customers, the portion likely to find themselves protected by the forces of competition most rapidly.

The elimination of restrictions on reselling and of limitations on interconnection would permit viable entry and operation in the arena by reselling firms. Those are the firms that take advantage of volume discounts, purchasing in bulk and then retailing at discount prices, to pass on to somewhat smaller customers some of the savings that competition brings to the 20 percent of local service customers with large volumes of usage.

In other areas of telecommunications, notably the markets served by the IXCs, such competition by resellers has been almost all that was needed to provide the benefits of competition to most other customer classes. For this purpose the regulator merely had to enforce the right of the resellers to purchase service on the same terms as those granted to other large customers. The resellers, who can enter the market quickly and with little sunk investment, act as retailers. Wherever the prices to large-volume subscribers are forced to low levels by competition, but the prices to smaller subscribers remain high, the resellers enter the market, purchase a large volume of service from an IXC at the favorable volume discounts that are available, and then undercut the IXC by reselling this service at a lower price to smaller-volume customers. Thus, resellers become the carriers who transmit the benign virus of competition from markets in which it is already present to those from which it is absent.

In the sale of access to households, however, this means of spreading the power of competition does not work, given the limitations of current technology. The reseller cannot carry out its retailing by carrying messages only to a few PBXs, as can be done in sales to a large-volume customer. If the retailer had to carry the messages via separate facilities individually constructed for each of its subscribers, its entry would require the expenditure of large sunk outlays, and that is an effective barrier to entry.

Resellers and the Interexchange Carriers. Discrimination in prices between interexchange carriers and other business customers, with higher prices to the former, means that the virus of competition has not yet been permitted to take over completely even that portion of the local arena. In part, this seems to be attributable to usage restrictions on resold services to the IXCs. Much of the problem can be ascribed to regulatory intervention in response to political pressures, making for the imposition and preservation of cross-subsidies, particularly to residential customers, with high access charges to the IXCs serving to help finance those cross-subsidies.

Competition Among Local Exchange Carriers. Competition is affecting the LECs in other ways as well. The first manifestation of direct competition is the provision of traditional local-loop service by private firms (other than carriers of television programs by cable) specializing entirely in telecommunications. In New Zealand the privatized telephone company, Telecom Corporation of New Zealand, Ltd., has been confronted by a rival, Clear Communications, Ltd., that is legally free to provide local-loop service of its own into the country's major cities, since New Zealand has no pure interexchange carriers.[5] The result will be one of overlapping LECs: while Clear must purchase access from Telecom, Telecom in turn will have to purchase access from Clear to complete calls to the latter's subscribers. If profitable operation of traditional, competing local loops by specialized telecommunications firms proves to be possible, prospects for effective competition in this arena will be enhanced in the United States as well.

Cable Telephony. The threat of competition has gone well beyond the possibility of resale, of bypass by large subscribers, and of direct rivalry between overlapping local exchange carriers. In part, this development is ascribable to technological progress. But its more immediate source is the growth of another set of enterprises that have already made the investment necessary to give them direct and widespread access to subscribers' premises—namely, suppliers of cable television service, which increasingly are reaching homes throughout the country. With some additional investment, the connections can be modified to permit those cable wires to carry telephone messages. Such "cable telephony" has already been introduced in the United Kingdom, where multichannel video programming is principally transmitted not by wire but by satellite to small home-receiver dishes. BT, formerly known as British Telecom and still the largest British telephone company, has expressed concern about the competitive threat posed by new cable television operators (in which American RBOCs have equity stakes), operators whose systems have more than enough bandwidth

---

5. *Clear Takes Telecom NZ Back to Court*, EXCHANGE, vol. 5, no. 5 (Feb. 12, 1993); *Clear and Telecom NZ Both Claim Victory in Local Access Case*, EXCHANGE, vol. 5, no. 1 (Jan. 15, 1993); Terry Hall, *From Monopoly to Competitor—New Zealand/Pacific Rim*, FIN. TIMES, Oct. 7, 1991, at § III (World Telecommunications), at 30. *See also* Telecom Corp. of New Zealand, Ltd. *v.* Clear Communications, Ltd., 3 N.Z.L.R. 247 (H.C. 1992).

(that is, transmission capacity) to provide telephone service as well as television service to residential users.[6]

Entry by the cable companies into the American local exchange markets has apparently been prevented principally by regulatory rules, but many informed observers believe that this exclusion cannot long continue. In January 1993, Time Warner, the second-largest cable multiple system operator (MSO) in the United States, announced that it will upgrade its cable television system in Orlando, Florida to be a "full-service network" capable of delivering video on demand in a manner technologically equivalent to offering an unlimited number of cable channels.[7] Employing digital compression and advanced technology for storage and retrieval of information and for signal switching, the system will provide interactive information services and, with further modifications, could offer conventional telephone service as well, if only it were permitted to do so by state and federal regulation.[8] In May 1993, Time Warner edged closer to its eventual provision of cable telecommunications when it announced that U S West, one of the seven RBOCs, would acquire a 25.5 percent interest in Time Warner's cable operations.[9]

Wireless Access and Full-Service Networks. The competitive prospects for cable telephony illustrate a larger phenomenon that surely will enhance competition in local telephone service, but at a future date that is difficult to predict. It has become a cliché to say that disparate techniques of telecommunications are "converging" in the sense that they permit us to transmit a particular message—whether it is a voice or a stream of data or a video image—by any of several different means. Thus, telephony, broadcasting, cable television, and mobile communications are fast becoming activities whose main difference is

6. *See* Raymond Snoddy, *BT Fears Threat of Cable Competitors*, FIN. TIMES, Oct. 16, 1992, at 9. *See also* ELI NOAM, TELECOMMUNICATIONS IN EUROPE 120–21 (Oxford Univ. Press 1992).

7. Johnnie L. Roberts & Mary Lu Carnevale, *Time Warner Plans Electronic "Superhighway,"* WALL ST. J., Jan. 27, 1993, at B10; TIME WARNER INC., 1992 FORM 10-K, at I-19 (1993).

8. Time Warner acknowledges already that its network "will be capable of providing . . . long distance telephone service," *id.*, by which the company presumably means local access for interexchange calls.

9. Laura Landro, Johnnie L. Roberts & Randall Smith, *Cable-Phone Link Is Promising Gamble: Time Warner Sees Synergy in Partnership*, WALL ST. J., May 18, 1993, at B1.

their regulatory treatment, rather than their technological or economic characteristics. Video programming can be delivered by conventional television broadcasters, or by direct broadcast satellite, cable, microwave, or telephone wires. Whatever the medium used, digital compression techniques now permit five or ten television signals to fit into the bandwidth currently occupied by one, thus vastly enhancing the capacity of the electromagnetic spectrum, once considered scarce, and allowing programmers to cater to the special tastes of narrow audiences. At the same time, the declining cost of computing has permitted greater decentralization of the processing and storage of information, in turn enabling the intelligence in the telecommunications network to reside to a greater extent in the dispersed customer premises equipment of ultimate users rather than the premises of some central provider of switching and transport. Accordingly, it is no longer appropriate to speak of a single public telephone network, but rather of a "network of networks," in which private communications networks, consisting of local-area networks (LANs) and wide-area networks (WANs), complement the public network or circumvent it entirely.[10]

Just as the airline industry transformed itself from a web of point-to-point routes to the hub-and-spoke system soon after deregulation, the market for the transmission and switching of voice, data, and video information is likely to undergo radical metamorphosis if permitted by regulators to do so. One market structure that may, plausibly, result entails a series of firms or consortia characterized by extensive vertical integration and economies of scope. Each such competitor will provide transmission (both local and long-distance), processing, storage, and switching of voice, data, and video to households, businesses, and mobile users. This rapidly evolving industry structure has been called "the vertical reintegration that divestiture attempted to dismantle."[11] Telecommunications firms appear to be approaching this common destination by very different routes that reflect not only the differences

---

10. For a concise and accessible survey of many of these technological developments, see JOSEPH A. PECAR, ROGER J. O'CONNOR & DAVID A. GARBIN, THE MCGRAW-HILL TELECOMMUNICATIONS FACTBOOK (McGraw-Hill, Inc. 1993).

11. HUBER, KELLOGG & THORNE, THE GEODESIC NETWORK II, *supra* note 3, at 1.38.

in technology employed, but also the differing nature and extent of the regulatory impediments to which these firms currently are subject.

In November 1992, McCaw Cellular Communications, the largest cellular telephone service provider in the United States, announced that 33 percent of the company would be acquired by AT&T, the largest interexchange carrier in the United States, and that AT&T also would receive the option eventually to acquire control of McCaw.[12] By August 1993, AT&T had announced that it would acquire 100 percent of McCaw.[13] The merger in effect recreates for certain markets a more technologically advanced version of the former Bell System: A fiber-optic interexchange network will be joined at each end by a wireless version of the local exchange, but one that, this time, faces substantial competition. The wireless access lines are, for the moment, still dependent on the LEC's wire-based local loop for switching. But the cost to AT&T and McCaw—which at the time of their November 1992 announcement had combined assets of $66 billion[14]—of installing their own switches does not seem insurmountable in relation to the benefits promised by creating their own wireless local exchange. By the late 1990s, the advent of personal communications services (PCS), such as pocket telephones, may significantly expand the opportunities for wireless local access.[15]

The Alternative Access Providers. Two logical pieces remain to be added to a consortium of the AT&T-McCaw variety—local fiber networks and cable facilities. The first of these is supplied by firms such as Teleport or MFS. These firms, known as alternative access

12. McCAW CELLULAR COMMUNICATIONS, INC., 1992 FORM 10-K, at 3 (1993). *See also* Mary Lu Carnevale, *AT&T-McCaw Link Stuns Baby Bells*, WALL ST. J., Nov. 6, 1992, at B1; John J. Keller, *Cellular Move Underscores AT&T's Transformation*, WALL ST. J., Nov. 6, 1992, at B1.

13. John J. Keller & Randall Smith, *AT&T Agrees to Buy McCaw Cellular In Stock Swap Valued at $12.6 Billion*, WALL ST. J., Aug. 17, 1993, at A3.

14. AMERICAN TELEPHONE & TELEGRAPH CO., 1992 ANNUAL REPORT 28 (1993); McCAW CELLULAR COMMUNICATIONS CORP., 1992 ANNUAL REPORT 21 (1993).

15. *See* GEORGE CALHOUN, WIRELESS ACCESS AND THE LOCAL TELEPHONE NETWORK 37–41 (Artech House, Inc. 1992). *See also* HUBER, KELLOGG & THORNE, THE GEODESIC NETWORK II, *supra* note 3, at 4.133–.135; Amendment of the Commission's Rules to Establish New Personal Communications Services, Tentative Decision & Mem. Op. & Order, Gen. Dkt. No. 90-314, 7 F.C.C. Rec. 7794 (1992); Telecom Corp. of New Zealand *v.* Commerce Comm'n, 3 N.Z.L.R. 429, 431–32 (C.A. 1992).

providers (ALTs) or competitive access providers (CAPs), have deployed modern optical fiber networks—sometimes called metropolitan-area networks (MANs)—throughout major cities.[16] They offer alternatives to the LEC facilities for direct transportation of high-volume traffic to the interexchange carriers and large business customers. Their activity has been concentrated in major office buildings and main switching locations for interexchange carriers. Recently there has also been growth of the arrangement called "expanded interconnection," also referred to as "collocation" in LEC central offices, that has created a new form of competition in the transportation of traffic by rivals from the LEC's central office to a carrier's pertinent location. In September 1992, the FCC ordered a large class of LECs throughout the country to provide such expanded interconnection.[17] This, too, will help undercut whatever market power remains in the local loop.

The second added piece required to make a full-service network, of course, is a cable television multiple system operator (MSO), whose broadband network of lines into households provides the capacity for delivery of voice and data in addition to video. It is no coincidence, therefore, that four of the six largest cable MSOs (TCI, Cox Enterprises, Continental Cablevision, and Comcast) own the majority of Teleport, one of the two leading CAPs—the local fiber networks that are complementary to the cable operators' facilities.

---

16. *See* MFS COMMUNICATIONS CO., PROSPECTUS FOR 8,000,000 SHARES (Apr. 21, 1993); Edmund L. Andrews, *The Local Call Goes up for Grabs,* N.Y. TIMES, Dec. 29, 1991, § 3 (Business), at 1 (discussing Teleport).

17. Expanded Interconnection with Local Telephone Company Facilities, Rep. & Order & Notice of Proposed Rulemaking, CC Dkt. Nos. 91-141, 92-222, 7 F.C.C. Rcd. 7369 (1992) (adopting rules for expanded interconnection for special access services). *See also* Expanded Interconnection with Local Telephone Company Facilities, Second Notice of Proposed Rulemaking, CC Dkt. Nos. 91-141, 80-286, 7 F.C.C. Rcd. 7740 (1992) (proposing rules for expanded interconnection for switched access); Transport Rate Structure and Pricing, Rep. & Order & Further Notice of Proposed Rulemaking, CC Dkt. No. 91-213, 7 F.C.C. Rcd. 7006 (1992) (addressing pricing under expanded interconnection).

The Regional Bell Operating Companies as Full-Service Networks

The seven RBOCs are also candidates for metamorphosis into full-service networks if two regulatory constraints are removed. One is the MFJ's line-of-business restriction that prohibits an RBOC from providing interLATA service.[18] The second is the provision in the Cable Communications Policy Act of 1984 prohibiting a LEC from providing video programming (that is, cable television) in its area of telephone service.[19] The practical effect of this second constraint is illustrated by Southwestern Bell's announcement in February 1993 that it will acquire the tenth-largest cable MSO, Hauser Communications. For Hauser is a firm whose service areas all lie outside Southwestern Bell's areas of wireline telephone service.[20]

Short of vacating of the MFJ and repeal of the cable-telco entry ban, how can the RBOCs achieve a metamorphosis into full-service networks? One way is through strategic use of constitutional litigation. In December 1992, Bell Atlantic sued the United States, challenging on First Amendment and other constitutional grounds the lawfulness of the statutory prohibition against a telephone company providing video programming in its telephone service area.[21] This lawsuit may prove to be the most significant litigation in telecommunications law since the 1940s, for Bell Atlantic, which has retained Professor Laurence Tribe of Harvard Law School and former Solicitor General Kenneth Starr as its advocates, has directly confronted the inferior protection that the Supreme Court has afforded electronic speech under the First Amendment. In August 1993, the United States District Court in Alexandria, Virginia sided with Bell Atlantic, ruling that the entry ban was unconstitutional both on its face and as applied to Bell Atlantic's specific circumstances.[22] As of this writing, the case is on appeal to

---

18. *See generally* KELLOGG, THORNE & HUBER, FEDERAL TELECOMMUNICATIONS LAW, *supra* note 2, at 295–314.

19. 47 U.S.C. § 533(b)(1).

20. Mark Robichaux & Mary Lu Carnevale, *Southwestern Bell Reaches Pact to Break Into Cable TV*, WALL ST. J., Feb. 10, 1993, at B1.

21. Chesapeake & Potomac Tel. Co. of Va. *v.* United States, No. 92-CV-1751 (E.D. Va. filed Dec. 17, 1992).

22. Chesapeake & Potomac Tel. Co. of Va. *v.* United States, 1993 U.S. Dist. LEXIS 11,822 (E.D. Va. Aug. 24, 1993).

the United States Court of Appeals for the Fourth Circuit. A subsequent appeal to the Supreme Court in 1994 or early 1995 seems inevitable.

A second way for the RBOCs to transform themselves into full-service networks is for them to divide themselves up voluntarily along the regulatory boundaries that have constrained their operation as multiproduct firms. In December 1992, the Pacific Telesis Group, a firm with more than $22 billion in assets, announced that it will split the company into two independently managed corporations in an untaxed distribution to shareholders.[23] One corporation will contain the regulated local telephone activities, and the other corporation, to which most of the senior management of the Pacific Telesis Group will migrate, will contain wireless services and unregulated activities.[24] The spinoff should free PacTel Wireless of all the restrictions that RBOCs face under the MFJ, including the prohibition on interLATA transmission, as well as the statutory ban on telephone company entry into cable.[25] PacTel Wireless could quickly, if imperfectly, replicate the AT&T-McCaw merger by acquiring or merging with one of AT&T's competitors in the interexchange market—MCI, Sprint, or LDDS. Of these three, Sprint already merged in March 1993 with Centel, a telephone company not formerly part of the Bell System (and thus not governed by the MFJ) that is considerably smaller than any of the RBOCs and that has relatively few cellular operations.[26] The Pacific Telesis spinoff would also free PacTel Wireless of the statutory prohibition against entering the cable television business. The disadvantage of the PacTel spinoff, of course, is that it destroys any economies of scope that may exist between the companies' wireline services and the businesses that PacTel Wireless will be free to enter.

---

23. PACIFIC TELESIS GROUP, 1992 FORM 10-K, at 4-10 (1993).

24. Mary Lu Carnevale, *Pacific Telesis Plan to Split Up Poses Challenges*, WALL ST. J., Dec. 12, 1992, at A3.

25. "It is expected that the spin-off will eliminate many of the financial, legal and regulatory constraints that have impeded the Corporation's efforts to grow and compete, including, for the wireless businesses, those restraints established as part of the Consent Decree." PACIFIC TELESIS GROUP, 1992 FORM 10-K, at 5 (1993). Another possible rationale for the PacTel spinoff is to foreclose the California Public Utilities Commission from one day requiring a unified Pacific Telesis Group to subsidize its local exchange customers with profits from its rapidly growing wireless businesses.

26. SPRINT CORP., 1992 ANNUAL REPORT 4 (1993).

In our discussion in Chapter 8 of regulatory barriers to entry, we will examine a third possible way for the RBOCs to become full-service networks. Under one possible alternative to the MFJ that deserves consideration, the RBOCs and other LECs would be permitted to enter currently prohibited lines of business under certain conditions; but, like the pricing rules to be discussed in Chapters 3 through 7, that regulatory regime would be designed to minimize the risk of cross-subsidy and predation until fully effective competition took hold, when the regime would become unnecessary but innocuous.

The Virtue of Built-in Adjustment Features for Regulatory Rules

Rules for regulating access and the other monopoly activities of the LECs, if they are to be more than transitory, must have considerable flexibility built into them. Because there are areas of activity in the industry in which effectiveness of competition is already claimed, and because almost everywhere competition may well grow and strengthen, rules that are appropriate only for monopoly services may be condemned to very brief lives. Much can be said for the design of regulations with automatic amendment processes that adapt themselves to changing market conditions. Otherwise, it may soon be necessary to redo entirely the costly, protracted, and painful process, now under way in the state regulatory agencies, to determine the rules for rational regulation of local and intrastate services suitable for current circumstances.

These rules must specify criteria that can be used to determine the degree to which competition has become effective in arenas proposed for partial or full deregulation. They must also incorporate suitable safeguards to ensure that deregulation is not abused. More on these topics will be said later in this monograph.

Conclusion: The Current State of Competition in Local Telephony

We have seen that in their dealings with large business customers the local exchange carriers already face rivalry by firms using wireless transmission techniques. If permitted to do so, cable television systems can provide two-way voice transmission into homes. Vertical integration can permit the creation of full-service suppliers that provide access service to the local market.

Thus, effective competition in some areas of local telephone service may well be here. We do not know yet whether substantial competition can prosper among the local exchange carriers that are often considered bastions of market power. Powerful rivalry may well emerge from many sources, given a suitable regulatory environment preventing acts that interfere with entry. But much of this competition is prospective.

Some local exchange carriers—such as Ameritech—seem to have recognized the inevitability (if not the imminence) of competition in the local loop and have offered to withdraw their opposition to new entrants before the state and federal regulatory agencies if suitable terms can be arranged.[27] At this point in the discussion, the pertinent conclusion is that the LECs can no longer feel confident that access service will remain immune from competition.

Although the local exchange carriers already face competition, little of it is directed to the operation of the local loop or access to it. A considerable part of the competition consists of rivalry between the LECs and the IXCs in intraLATA toll service. There is also competition in centrex service, as a substitute for customer-owned PBX facilities, in coin phone service, and in terminal equipment. The competition has begun to invade the primary sources of regulatory concern in local telephony. Yet, until the regulatory program moves toward freedom of entry and elimination of impediments to competition, we can expect the current state of affairs to continue. The signs are encouraging, however, to those who favor a market mechanism that guides matters so that competition grows where it can and serves as a model for regulation in those portions of local activity where competition does not prove to be viable. For regulation is indeed moving toward freedom of entry, and toward the sorts of rules favored by the preponderance of economists concerned with regulatory issues.

---

27. Petition of Ameritech for Declaratory Ruling and Related Waivers to Establish a New Regulatory Model for the Ameritech Region (filed before the FCC Mar. 1, 1993).

3

Regulating Local Telecommunications: Some Basic Principles

THIS CHAPTER SEEKS to describe the principles upon which economists base their recommendations for regulation of telecommunications pricing and related subjects. It examines such criteria as economic efficiency, perfect competition, Ramsey pricing rules, and pricing in perfectly contestable markets, all of which bear some relation to promotion of the general welfare.

Our discussion of regulation will generally be confined to *economic regulation*, as distinguished from *health and safety regulation*. The latter includes such variegated concerns as the purity of food and drugs, the minimization of sources of accidents in the workplace, and environmental protection. Although these concerns have economic implications, they are not central to the regulations that concern us here. Economic regulation deals with variables and modes of behavior that are directly economic—decisions on pricing, market entry, investment, outlays on research and development, and the like. In what follows, the unmodified term "regulation" always connotes economic regulation as that expression has just been interpreted.

The Pareto Criterion of Economic Efficiency

We presume here that the sole objective of economic regulation is to achieve "economic efficiency"—that state of affairs in which, as the specialized literature of welfare economics recognizes, no opportunity to promote the general welfare has been neglected. Such an opportunity is defined as the availability of a course of action that will benefit at least some individuals, in their own estimation, in a way not achieved at the expense of others. Such an action constitutes a "Pareto improvement," named after Vilfredo Pareto, to whom the concept is often ascribed.[1] Clearly, the neglect of any Pareto-superior opportunity means that the economy has forgone the chance to make some people better off without harming anyone. A policy adopted by a regulatory agency is, then, deemed to be consistent with economic efficiency if no feasible change in that program promises to constitute a Pareto improvement. This absence of any unused opportunities for Pareto improvements is said to constitute Pareto optimality. As we will see, the apparently innocuous criterion of Pareto optimality is in fact much more powerful than it seems. It is capable of generating as unexpected and sophisticated rules as those entailed in the theory of Ramsey pricing, to be discussed below.

The criterion of economic efficiency is by no means accepted universally. Even where regulatory agencies vow unswerving allegiance to the principle—or to its functional equivalent, the competitive-market model—their subsequent courses of action often serve only to undermine it. Indeed, virtually every regulatory agency operates under a legislative mandate listing an extensive set of objectives that have little to do with economic efficiency and that sometimes conflict with that goal. Many of those legislated principles invite dismissal as mere platitudes—proclamations of devotion to (undefined) virtue and undeviating patriotism. But others go beyond that, taking stances to which economists are in no position to object.[2]

---

1. For a succinct nontechnical discussion of Pareto efficiency, see B. Lockwood, *Pareto Efficiency*, *in* 3 THE NEW PALGRAVE DICTIONARY OF ECONOMICS 811–13 (John Eatwell, Murray Milgate & Peter Newman, eds., Macmillan Press Limited 1987). For a more mathematical treatment, see DAVID M. KREPS, A COURSE IN MICROECONOMIC THEORY 153–56 (Princeton Univ. Press 1990).

2. The principle of economic efficiency itself has even been questioned. Writing for a majority of the Supreme Court in the *Ingot Molds Case*, American Commercial Lines, Inc. *v.* Louisville & Nashville R.R., 392 U.S. 574, 586–89 n.16 (1968), the late Justice Marshall took issue with one of the present authors on just this subject and asked tellingly whether a change that benefits one group but neither harms nor benefits another may not reasonably be considered objectionable and grossly unfair by the latter. For a critique of the decision, see RICHARD A. POSNER, ECONOMIC ANALYSIS

Typically, for example, the principle that special provision should be made for the welfare of the indigent and the incapacitated receives some commitment. The provision of "lifeline telephone services"—that is, basic service without frills at bargain rates to a set of subscribers who qualify—is a nearly universal consequence. Economists can rationally object to the method usually selected to finance such special services: why should they be paid for by other telephone subscribers, rather than by the public as a whole from the government treasury? Yet political practicalities can preclude any other arrangement. Lifeline service, though meritorious, hardly qualifies as a Pareto improvement. It clearly benefits one group, the indigent, but at the expense of those providing the subsidy required to cover the cost.

Another example of a goal that conflicts with economic efficiency is the nearly ubiquitous target called "universal service." The idea is to make telecommunications services available to everyone, with no group excluded because of the costliness of serving its members. Thus, the opening sentence of the Communications Act of 1934 established the FCC "to make available, so far as possible, to all the people of the United States a rapid, efficient, Nation-wide, and world-wide wire and radio communication service with adequate facilities at reasonable charges."[3] For years before the advent of competition undermined the system, subsidies were openly extracted from urban customers and from customers using especially busy routes, with their characteristically low marginal costs attributable to scale economies. This made it possible to supply service at low prices to farmers in isolated areas and to others in sparsely settled locations.[4] Competition undermined this arrangement because entrants initially specialized in supplying service to customers served by those high-density routes that were overpriced. The competitors could underprice the incumbent supplier on these routes and still make a profit. Thus, the source of the subsidy to isolated subscribers was eroded by competition. Despite the incumbents' predictable denuncia-

OF LAW 356 (Little, Brown & Co., 4th ed. 1992).

3. 47 U.S.C. § 151.

4. *See* PAUL W. MACAVOY, INDUSTRY REGULATION AND THE PERFORMANCE OF THE AMERICAN ECONOMY 15–17 (W.W. Norton & Co. 1992).

tion of this pattern of entry as "cream skimming," it did serve economic efficiency. At the same time, however, it acted as an impediment to universal service.

One can cite still other objectives that conflict with economic efficiency. One of the most significant in telecommunications regulation, which we will discuss in Chapter 8, has been the sometimes unacknowledged desire to ensure the survival of entrants, even those who are inefficient suppliers, so that their high-cost products can continue to be supplied. Often this is accomplished at the consumer's expense.

Despite these supplementary or conflicting objectives, economists who testify on regulatory issues continue to place primary emphasis on the criterion of economic efficiency, and some proceed as though it were the only defensible goal. There are several reasons for this. First, this premise has proven to be a powerful analytic tool, often yielding concrete and unambiguous recommendations for policy. This foundation clearly underlies the substantial measure of agreement among economist witnesses in recent years, even among those testifying on behalf of clients on opposite sides of cases. All these witnesses surely consider themselves to be dedicated to the public interest, and their general recommendations coincide because the principle of economic efficiency implies what courses of action will serve the general welfare most effectively. Second, the principle of economic efficiency is persuasive in itself, and derives further persuasiveness from the fact that the competitive-market model calls for courses of action identical to those required for economic efficiency.

Thus, in the pages that follow we will use the phrase "the public interest" more precisely and restrictively than do the Communications Act, the FCC, and the state public utility commissions. It will connote economic efficiency, or the maximization of the general welfare of consumers and producers—that is, the maximization of the sum of consumers' surplus and producers' surplus. Often this criterion is referred to in the abbreviated form "consumer welfare maximization."

The primacy that economists ascribe to economic efficiency and consumer welfare maximization has a related benefit: it harmonizes economic regulation and antitrust law. For in the latter, the Supreme Court has contributed a muscular jurisprudence asserting that the first goal of the Sherman Act and other federal antitrust statutes is to be a "consumer welfare prescription."[5] This harmony between regulation and antitrust has three important implications. First, the same basic tools of microeconomic analysis can be employed in one as in the other. There can be little disagreement that the economic sophistication of antitrust law has enriched the regulatory analysis of natural monopoly. Second, changes in technology or other circumstances that permit natural monopoly to give way to competition impart continuity to the relationship between economic regulation and antitrust. Third, many of the thorniest problems in antitrust law—such as judicial enforcement of injunctive remedies under the MFJ or the essential facilities doctrine—are fundamentally regulatory in nature, involving issues such as entry or the pricing of intermediate goods sold to competitors. Thus, the economic scholarship on regulation can in many instances enrich antitrust jurisprudence.[6]

The Competitive-Market Standard for Economic Regulation

A second standard for economic regulation, one directly related to economic efficiency, commands nearly universal acceptance among noneconomists and economists alike. This standard holds that the proper task of economic regulation is to intervene where competitive forces are too weak to defend the public interest unaided, with regulation undertaking to restrict or prevent behavior, inadvertent or deliberate, that threatens to damage the public interest because it deviates from what effective competition would have permitted, had it been present. This criterion is the *competitive-market standard* for regulation. It stems from the view that arenas in which competition is

5. National Collegiate Athletic Ass'n. *v.* Board of Regents of Univ. of Okla., 468 U.S. 85, 107 (1984); Reiter *v.* Sonotone Corp., 442 U.S. 330, 343 (1979) (citing ROBERT H. BORK, THE ANTITRUST PARADOX: A POLICY AT WAR WITH ITSELF 66 (Free Press 1978)).

6. *See* Stephen G. Breyer, *Antitrust, Deregulation, and the Newly Liberated Marketplace*, 75 CALIF. L. REV. 1005 (1987).

pervasive and vigorous are best left to fend for themselves without governmental intrusion, both because competition is a powerful protector of the public interest and because regulation has heavy costs. These costs include the direct expenses of administration and compliance and the indirect burdens of the ancillary consequences for economic efficiency.

The competitive-market standard asserts that the regulator's task is to serve as a proxy for competition—to stand *in loco competitio*, preventing all actions that competition would have precluded, and requiring all courses of economic behavior that competition would have imposed. From this view there follow three guiding principles for the regulator:

1. Where competitive forces are adequate and effective, the regulator should eschew all forms of intervention.

2. The regulator should study the courses of behavior that a competitive market imposes. The regulator then should impose such behavior upon the regulated firm in markets where competition is inadequate to protect the public interest—for example, by requiring the firm to set prices as it would have been forced to do by market pressures if competition had been effective. This principle requires a study of how firms would behave in the given technological and other circumstances if the competitive pressures generated by fully unimpeded and costless entry and exit, contrary to fact, were to prevail.

3. The regulator should not restrict decisions any further than this, and the regulated firm should be left free to pursue any course of action that effective competitive-market forces would have permitted, had they been present.

A number of regulatory agencies have moved toward acceptance of these three principles. Much of the testimony that they have heard from economist witnesses has examined the principles of competitive behavior, described how competitive markets work, and discussed, for example, what prices such markets impose for final products, for partly used assets of a firm, and for intermediate inputs sold by one firm to another. The witnesses then generally agree that it is appropriate for regulators to impose exactly the same course of behavior upon the regulated firm.

Economists, however, arrive at this competitive-market model by a different route from the one described at the beginning of this section. They do not simply proceed from the assumption that competition is inherently virtuous and therefore should serve as the regulatory standard. Rather, economists generally start from their dedication to economic efficiency; then they accept competition as a suitable model for regulation on the basis of rigorous arguments showing that, in the absence of governmental interference and externalities,[7] competitive markets will always elicit behavior by firms and individuals consistent with the requirements of economic efficiency. The roots of this observation extend at least to Adam Smith, and its full and rigorous derivation was provided in the 1950s, in the well-known writings of Kenneth Arrow and Gerard Debreu.[8]

We need not review the details of the Arrow-Debreu theorem, because its pertinence to economic regulation is limited. Its main implications for our purposes are that in equilibrium in a perfectly competitive market production will always be carried out only by firms that can do so with lowest costs; that inputs will always be

---

7. An externality is an unintended consequence of a course of action that incidentally has beneficial or detrimental effects upon third parties, from whom the generator of the externalities cannot collect adequate compensation if the externalities are beneficial, or to whom compensation for damage will not automatically be paid by the generator if they are detrimental. *See, e.g.*, WILLIAM J. BAUMOL & WALLACE E. OATES, THE THEORY OF ENVIRONMENTAL POLICY 14–21 (Cambridge Univ. Press 2d ed. 1988). The emission of smoke by an electricity-generating station is the standard example, and the third-party victims can include persons different from both the suppliers of the electricity and their customers. Such an externality is a source of inefficiency, because the generator of the externality does not pay for the social costs imposed by the actions, and will therefore have no market incentive to reduce the damaging emissions.

8. *See* Kenneth J. Arrow, *An Extension of the Basic Theorems of Classical Welfare Economics, in* PROCEEDINGS OF THE SECOND BERKELEY SYMPOSIUM ON MATHEMATICAL STATISTICS AND PROBABILITY 507 (Jerzy Neyman ed., Univ. of California Press 1951); Gerard Debreu, *The Coefficient of Resource Utilization,* 19 ECONOMETRICA 273 (1951); *see also* GERARD DEBREU, THEORY OF VALUE: AN AXIOMATIC ANALYSIS OF ECONOMIC EQUILIBRIUM (Yale Univ. Press 1959).

allocated among firms in a way consistent with economic efficiency in production; and that output quantities will always be tailored to the preferences of consumers, and will consequently never fail to take advantage of an opportunity to introduce a Pareto improvement. This final implication of Pareto optimality holds because, in such markets, prices are set so that firms can avoid losses only by acting in the manner just described. With their belief in the value of economic efficiency, economists are driven to accept the competitive-market standard for regulation, because competition serves as the viable instrument capable of moving the economy toward their ideal.

One other feature of perfect competition contributing to its acceptance by noneconomists as a regulatory guide is the profit level implied by equilibrium in a perfectly competitive market. As is emphasized in every economics textbook, in such an equilibrium the firm is condemned to earn (no more than) zero economic profit, and it can only attain this level of profit—that is, it can avoid outright loss—by achieving perfect efficiency in its operation and by charging prices sufficiently low to avoid driving its customers into the arms of its rivals. The zero-economic-profit requirement is not so draconian as it sounds, because it is defined to include gross earnings sufficient to pay interest to those who have lent funds to the firm and to provide a return to equity holders that is consistent with the prevailing level of interest payments, after adjusting for differences in the risk of debt and equity. Nevertheless, this level of earnings permitted by competitive-market forces limits earnings to what is called the cost of capital, or to what regulators traditionally have called a "fair rate of return."[9] In other words, besides serving as an instrument for attaining economic efficiency, perfect competition promises fairness by its preclusion of profits that might be deemed excessive. This guarantee of fairness, then, is another reason for the widespread acceptance of the competitive-market standard for regulation.

The competitive-market standard, however, frequently gives rise to a rather primitive error. Often, a witness at a regulatory hearing who has finished expositing principles of competitive-market behavior

---

9. *See, e.g.*, 1 ALFRED E. KAHN, THE ECONOMICS OF REGULATION: PRINCIPLES AND INSTITUTIONS 42–45 (MIT Press rev. ed. 1988).

finds the argument countered by an opposing witness: "What you have just heard is all very well, and there is no question that competitive-market behavior is desirable. But the local telephone market [or whatever market happens to be at issue] is clearly anything but competitive. Therefore, the materials just provided by my opponent are unrealistic and irrelevant." The fallacy of this retort, of course, is its failure to recognize that the competitive-market standard is designed to guide regulation *only* in markets that are *not* competitive. As we have noted, in markets that *are* competitive, the standard counsels regulators to stay away, not to intrude. It is precisely and exclusively in noncompetitive markets that regulatory intrusion is justified. That is, the competitive market-standard derives its relevance only from the choice of noncompetitive markets as those requiring regulation.

But Which Form of Competition?

A significant shortcoming of the foregoing discussion is its reliance on the theoretical model of perfect competition. That is the model most closely examined in formal economics, and the one whose relation to the requirements of economic efficiency has been studied most extensively. Because economists agree that equilibrium in perfect competition entails efficiency and Pareto optimality, if only government interference and externalities are absent, it is natural that the competitive model in its theoretical form should suggest itself as the proper guide for regulation. That model, however, has several critical, unavoidable attributes that render it inapplicable to issues of economic regulation in general, and to those related to local telephone service in particular. Consequently, the model frequently has been replaced by two equally theoretical concepts—the Ramsey model and the model of perfect contestability.

The model of perfect competition has two related attributes that limit its applicability to regulation. First, the market must be populated by a large number of firms, each of which is too small to influence prices. The firms must all be passive "takers" of the prices imposed on them by the impersonal forces of the market. Second, by its nature, competitive equilibrium entails local constant returns to scale—that is, neither economies nor diseconomies of scale in the neighborhood of any equilibrium point. This means that at such a point a small and equal percentage increase in all input quantities must just suffice to increase all outputs by the same percentage.[10]

Each of these features virtually rules out the applicability of the perfect-competition model to issues in economic regulation, at least in the field of telecommunications. By the nature of its purpose, economic regulation rarely is employed in fields of activity populated by a multiplicity of minuscule firms. Regulation addresses phenomena such as monopoly and market power, and the many-small-firm assumption of perfect competition is designed to eliminate the possibility of just such attributes in a market. Moreover, in the industries subject to regulation, scale economies are likely to be present, and not merely through happenstance. The availability of economies of scale and scope—that is, economies made possible by multiproduct production—is a powerful source of competitive advantage to larger firms, which can thereby produce more cheaply than their smaller rivals. In other words, regulation characteristically intrudes in industries in which at least some firms are big, and that is most likely where economies of scale prevail.

These two features of the model of perfect competition do not by themselves disqualify the model from application. After all, the purpose of regulation is to require noncompetitive firms to conform to the behavior of an unrealistic model. Thus the mere fact that perfect competition is unrealistic does not render the model inappropriate for use by the regulator. Rather, the model is inappropriate because the actions that it counsels the regulator to take are neither feasible nor desirable.

---

10. *See, e.g.,* HAL R. VARIAN, MICROECONOMIC ANALYSIS 14–17 (W.W. Norton & Co., 3d ed. 1992).

Marginal-Cost Pricing and the Need to Depart from It

Specifically, when regulators seek guidance on pricing rules for a regulated firm, the competitive model tells them to require price to equal marginal cost, the well-known pricing principle that characterizes competitive equilibrium. The marginal cost of a product X is defined as the addition to the firm's total outlays that results when the output of X is increased by a very small amount. (In mathematical terms, it is the derivative of total cost with respect to the output of X.) Under perfect competition, as we have seen, price is set outside the firm by market forces. The firm observes that price and adapts its output quantities to that price figure, choosing the output volume that maximizes profit at the given price. (Recall that zero economic profit is the most that the perfectly competitive firm can expect to earn in the long run, so that it has no option but to seek to maximize profit if it is to avoid insolvency.) But if the firm's output is such that marginal cost is less than the given price, then the profit-maximizing firm must increase its output, thereby adding to its profit the difference between the price and the marginal cost of the incremental output units. This process of expansion ends only when the diminishing returns assumed to prevail in perfect competition have raised the marginal cost of further increases in output X to the level of the market-determined price of X. At that point, further increases in output clearly will add no more to profit. Hence, in competitive equilibrium, price and marginal costs will always end up in equality.

Economic efficiency requires the price of every product to be set equal to its marginal cost, provided that doing so is consistent with the economic viability of the firm (which will be true in the absence of scale economies). This can be verified directly from what has already been said here, since it has been noted that perfect competition yields equilibria that are efficient, and that the prices entailed by these perfectly competitive equilibria are equal to marginal costs and yield zero economic profits.

A more direct way of viewing the matter is to interpret marginal cost as the true cost a consumer imposes upon an economy in buying an additional unit of product. Thus, if price is set equal to marginal cost, the costs of the purchase to the consumer and to society must be the same. As a result, if the consumer makes purchase decisions rationally, achieving a given level of satisfaction at minimum cost to himself, he automatically does so at minimum cost to society, as economic efficiency requires. If prices are not set equal to marginal costs, inefficiencies are induced in a manner that is easy to see. Suppose product X has a marginal cost 10 percent lower than Y's, but the price of Y is lower than that of X. Then a consumer who is indifferent between the two goods can be expected to select Y, the item with the lower price, even though its production uses up resources more valuable than those needed to produce X.

Adherence to this well-known principle of marginal-cost pricing, on the belief that it maximizes the general welfare, can lead regulators astray, however. For it is equally well known that if the firm's production process is subject to economies of scale, then the requirement that prices be set equal to marginal costs is a recipe for bankruptcy. Under economies of scale, the revenues yielded by marginal-cost pricing will necessarily fall short of the total costs of the firm's outputs.[11] An easy way to see this proposition intuitively is to recognize that substantial fixed costs are a primary source of scale economies because the fixed cost per unit of output obviously falls when output increases (the "spreading of overheads"). By its very definition, however, fixed cost is a cost whose amount does not change when output varies. Hence, a price equal to marginal cost, which is *the addition* to total cost resulting from an output change, cannot include any contribution to fixed cost. Other things being equal, marginal cost stays precisely the same, whether fixed costs are large, small, or zero. Consequently, prices that cover only marginal costs cannot be expected to cover fixed costs as well.

Thus, no regulator can be expected to follow the precept of marginal-cost pricing that is integral to the model of perfect competition, for to do so would either drive the regulated firm into bankruptcy or force government permanently to subsidize the result-

---

11. *See, e.g.*, KENNETH E. TRAIN, OPTIMAL REGULATION: THE ECONOMIC THEORY OF NATURAL MONOPOLY 14–15 (MIT Press 1991); DENNIS W. CARLTON & JEFFREY M. PERLOFF, MODERN INDUSTRIAL ORGANIZATION 796–98 (Scott, Forseman/Little, Brown Higher Education 1990).

ing deficit. If the model of perfect competition cannot offer the regulator useful guidance on price regulation, it is virtually worthless as a model for an agency charged with regulating prices.

More than that, the model of perfect competition turns regulation and antitrust toward attempts to populate the industry with a multiplicity of smaller enterprises. But where scale economies are present and substantial, such an effort cannot long succeed unless government virtually dictates all operations of the firms. For otherwise, any one firm that happens to expand will reap a competitive advantage through the scale economies that become available to it, and it will thereby be able to expand even further, all at the expense of its smaller rivals. Thus, where scale economies are substantial an equilibrium with many small firms cannot be expected to last. Nor is it in the social interest that such an equilibrium should endure. For in an equilibrium with scale economies, costs will be unnecessarily high if all enterprises are tiny, since the smallness of the firms must prevent them from taking advantage of the cost savings that scale economies offer. With costs unnecessarily high, prices must be correspondingly excessive if the firm is to survive. That is, the small scale of firms, in equilibrium, can be achieved only at the expense of consumers, who must forgo the savings from the scale economies that would be passed along through lower prices. That result is hardly consonant with the goal of economic efficiency.

The Ramsey Solution

One alternative source of guidance for economic regulation is the body of analysis now called "Ramsey theory," the formal structure first laid out for the analysis of tax policy by the young Cambridge philosopher Frank Ramsey, who managed to produce revolutionary contributions to probability theory, combinatorial analysis, geometry, and economics, as well as to his own field, before his death at age twenty-six. Since its formulation, the theory has elicited contributions by such distinguished economists as A.C. Pigou, Paul Samuelson, Marcel Boiteux, John Hicks, Peter Diamond, and John Mirrlees, and the validity of its arguments seems to command universal acceptance among economists.[12]

Applied to the field of regulation, Ramsey theory undertakes to determine those second-best prices that are Pareto-optimal, subject to the requirement that they yield revenues sufficient to cover the total costs incurred by the supplier of the products in question. That is, recognizing that in the presence of scale economies a firm would lose money if required to set the prices of each of its products equal to the corresponding marginal costs, the theory explores the alternative pricing possibilities. In a multiproduct firm, many combinations of prices will just enable the supplier to cover its total cost. Ramsey analysis undertakes to determine which of these price sets maximizes economic welfare—or, what turns out to be the same thing, which price set is consistent with Pareto optimality, subject to the requirement that the prices yield revenues adequate for the firm to cover all its costs.

Ramsey analysis provides a set of mathematical formulas that can be solved, with the aid of the appropriate cost and demand data, to determine precisely what prices are required to achieve second-best optimality. This calculation would appear to deprive the regulated firm of any vestige of freedom in its pricing decisions. Apparently the regulator simply calculates the Ramsey-optimal prices from the formulas and directs the regulated firm to adopt those prices and no others. Taken in this way, Ramsey theory is hardly to be interpreted as an instrument of deregulation—that is, a means to enhance the freedom of decision making by the management of the regulated firm. Undoubtedly, some regulators have been tempted to interpret the role of Ramsey theory in this way. Generally, however, the analysis has been assigned a more modest role in regulatory practice. To understand the limitedness of the role it has usually been assigned, we must review what the analysis asserts.

---

12. The original paper is Frank Ramsey, *A Contribution to the Theory of Taxation*, 37 ECON. J. 47 (1927). For a review of the subsequent literature, see William J. Baumol, *Ramsey Pricing*, in 4 THE NEW PALGRAVE DICTIONARY OF ECONOMICS, *supra* note 1, at 49–51; William J. Baumol & David F. Bradford, *Optimal Departures From Marginal Cost Pricing*, 60 AM. ECON. REV. 265 (1970).

First, although Ramsey analysis is invoked most frequently for the case of scale economies, its results apply equally whether there are scale economies, diseconomies, or constant returns to scale. Second, the Ramsey formula most frequently cited—the so-called inverse-elasticity formula—is a special case that is *not* applicable universally. It holds only when the set of products at issue contains no two items that are substitutes (like Coca-Cola and Pepsi-Cola) or complements (like bread and butter) in demand.[13]

The logic of the Ramsey formula is intuitively explainable from the proposition that, if it were feasible financially, economic welfare would be maximized by setting the price of each product equal to its marginal cost. If this set of prices yields revenues insufficient to cover the supplier's total cost, however, the prices must be modified for the goods to continue to be supplied by private enterprise. But every deviation of price from marginal cost creates some inefficiency—first, because it provides an incentive for consumers to switch to those goods whose prices are raised only modestly relative to their true marginal cost, and second, because every rise in price restricts demand by cutting into consumer purchasing power.

The objective, then, is to revise prices in the way that minimizes the need to deviate from marginal costs, while eliciting the requisite increase in total revenue of the firm—that is, raise most the prices of those items that yield the largest revenue contribution, or the most "bang for the buck." This rule immediately yields the course of action prescribed by Ramsey theory. If good X has a large price elasticity of demand—that is, a 1 percent rise in its price severely cuts demand—then a rise in the price of X will add little to the firm's revenue. But if the demand for good Y is inelastic, then a 1 percent

---

13. The prices that will emerge under the regulatory rules proposed in this monograph will not necessarily be Ramsey prices. Indeed, in theory these may differ altogether. There is reason to expect, however, that in practice the prices that would have emerged, had competition been fully effective, will tend to approximate the Ramsey prices. Indeed, even in theory, because those competitive prices will be the prices required for economic efficiency if two or more firms are present in the market, they must be the same as the pertinent Ramsey prices. For proofs that these competitive (contestable) market prices must be efficient in multifirm equilibria, see WILLIAM J. BAUMOL, JOHN C. PANZAR & ROBERT D. WILLIG, CONTESTABLE MARKETS AND THE THEORY OF INDUSTRY STRUCTURE, chaps. 2–5, 11, 12 (Harcourt Brace Jovanovich, rev. ed. 1988).

rise in its price will cut only modestly into the quantity of *Y* demanded, and so will add a comparatively great amount toward eliminating the shortfall in the firm's revenue.

Hence, the damage to welfare is minimized if the shortfall is covered through smaller increases in the prices of the goods whose demands are elastic, and larger increases in the prices of goods whose demands are comparatively inelastic. This pricing rule, in essence, is the logic of the inverse-elasticity formula, which states that, where goods are neither substitutes nor complements, the percentage difference between the price of any good *X* and the marginal cost of *X* should be inversely proportionate to the price elasticity of demand for *X*. A formal derivation of the inverse-elasticity formula appears as Appendix 3–1 to this chapter.

Where some of the firm's products are complements, substitutes, or a mixture of the two, in addition to the own-price elasticities of demand, the cross-price elasticities also become pertinent. That is, the effect of a change in the price of good *X* on the quantity demanded of another good *Y* also matters directly. Where commodity demands are interrelated in such ways, an attempt to increase revenue by raising the price of *X* can either be frustrated by an accompanying fall in the quantity of *Y* demanded, or the price rise can overshoot its mark if the indirect effect on demand goes in the opposite direction. Therefore, to use the full Ramsey analysis to calculate second-best optimal prices, one needs information on the marginal cost of, and the own-price elasticity of demand for, each of the products in question. One probably needs to know the full set of cross-price elasticities as well.

This data requirement is one reason why most regulators and consulting economists have rejected the use of the Ramsey formulas even to provide approximations for the prices that the regulated firm should be permitted to charge for its products.[14] Marginal-cost

---

14. Another reason why regulators reject a regime of Ramsey pricing is the inelasticity of demand for local telephone service, which means that the price of such service is likely to be increased substantially by the Ramsey rules. It is thought that the resulting reduction in demand, though smaller in relative terms than the reduction in demand for more price-elastic services, would tend to frustrate the universal-service goal in telecommunications regulation.

figures are difficult enough to come by, although reasonably defensible approximations have been provided by firms to regulatory bodies. But up-to-date estimates of the full set of pertinent elasticities and cross-elasticities are virtually impossible to calculate, particularly in markets where demand conditions change frequently and substantially. As a result, an attempt to provide the regulator with an extensive set of Ramsey prices is likely to be beset by inaccuracies, by obsolete demand data, and by delays that will prevent the firm from responding promptly and appropriately to evolving market conditions.

Rather, regulators have accepted the usefulness of Ramsey theory as a source of general qualitative guidance rather than as a generator of precise and definitive prescriptions for pricing. Ramsey theory has, for example, been used to defend the legitimacy in terms of the general welfare of what in the regulatory arena is called "differential pricing"—that is, the use of discriminatory prices, in the economic rather than the legal sense.[15] After all, the Ramsey formula is a prescription for deriving those prices whose deviations from marginal costs will serve the public interest where scale economies are present. But such differentiated price-marginal cost deviations are precisely what economists mean by the term "price discrimination." Ramsey theory has also been used to reject high markups on costs in the prices of goods whose demands are highly elastic, and to note that the self-interest of firms will normally lead them to avoid that sort of pricing behavior, in the understanding that charging high prices for goods whose demands are elastic is a sure way to lose one's customers.[16] In sum, Ramsey-pricing analysis continues to play a significant role in regulation, and one that may become more substantial in the future. But that role is nevertheless circumscribed, and Ramsey analysis is unlikely to determine the actual magnitudes of regulated prices.

15. *See, e.g.*, National Rural Telecom Ass'n *v.* FCC, 988 F.2d 174, 182–83 (D.C. Cir. 1993) (Williams, J.); Policy and Rules Concerning Rates for Dominant Carriers, Further Notice of Proposed Rulemaking, CC Dkt. No. 87-313, 3 F.C.C. Rec. 3195, 3257-58 ¶¶ 111–15 (1988).

16. *See, e.g.*, Coal Rate Guidelines, Nationwide, 1 I.C.C.2d 520, 526–27 (1985).

One final aspect of Ramsey analysis merits attention. In a competitive market, the own-price elasticity of demand is considerably smaller for a product than for a firm. If a firm unilaterally raises its price for a product, it will lose customers to other sellers, even if those customers are not lost to the industry. Which of these two elasticity figures should be used in the Ramsey formula? The industry elasticity is often assumed to be the appropriate one, but that is not generally correct. The purpose of the Ramsey calculation is to bring to the firm the addition to total revenue that it needs to cover its costs, and to do so with minimal deviation of prices from marginal costs. The way to do so is to focus upon changes in those prices for which a given percentage increase contributes most to the firm's revenues. But the prices that will accomplish this objective are those for which *the firm's* demand elasticity is lowest, regardless of what the own-price elasticity of demand may be for those products for the entire industry.[17] This observation is important. It means that Ramsey markups on competitive products will be lower, because they are appropriately guided by the firm's elasticity of demand; to compensate for this, Ramsey markups on monopoly products will be higher than they would be if the pertinent demand elasticity for each of the firm's products were that of the industry.

The Endogeneity of the Demand Elasticity for a Regulated Firm

Application of Ramsey analysis to regulation is subject to another important caveat because feasibility of the calculations is likely to require them to take the pertinent demand elasticities as a given. In the language of economics, these elasticities are then treated as exogenous. But regulators considerably influence the firm's demand elasticity by their decisions and policies that affect the firm's actual or potential competitors. Clearly, severe constraint of firms' entry and pricing will somewhat immunize each enterprise from the competitive

---

17. A review of the simplified derivation of the Ramsey formula in Appendix 3-1 to this chapter confirms that the marginal revenue, and hence the demand elasticities, throughout the mathematical argument are indeed those for the firm, not those for the industry.

pressures of others. That immunity from competition will reduce the elasticity of each supplier's demand—that is, it will reduce the loss of business that results from a rise in its prices.[18] The firm's price elasticity of demand thus must be said to be endogenously determined by the regulatory process itself. With such regulatorily influenced demand elasticities, it is not clear that Ramsey prices calculated *ex ante* will be those necessary for economic efficiency.

It appears especially clear in telecommunications that a firm's price elasticity of demand is endogenously determined by its regulatory environment. At least five kinds of regulatory barriers to entry or pricing contribute to this:

1. Federal regulation constrains entry into various segments of the telecommunications industry, not merely in local telephony, often in the name of promoting "diversity of expression." These statutory and regulatory barriers include the newspaper-television cross-ownership rule;[19] the statutory prohibition on a telephone company's provision of video programming (that is, cable television) within its area of telephone service;[20] the regulatory barrier to cross-ownership of a television network and a cable television system;[21] the foreign ownership restrictions in the Communications Act;[22] the financial interest and syndication rules restricting television network entry into program production and ownership;[23] and regulations that limit the horizontal scale of a television or radio broadcasting firm (and thus limit its ability to enter new markets without divesting itself of stations elsewhere).[24]

---

18. For a formal derivation of how a firm's own-price elasticity of demand is affected by the ease or difficulty of entry—known as the price elasticity of supply for the competitive fringe—see William E. Landes & Richard A. Posner, *Market Power in Antitrust Cases,* 94 HARV. L. REV. 937, 945 (1981).

19. 47 C.F.R. § 73.3555(c).

20. 47 U.S.C. § 533(b)(1).

21. 47 C.F.R. § 76.501(a)(1).

22. 47 U.S.C. § 310(b).

23. 47 C.F.R. § 73.658(j). *But see* Schurz Comm., Inc. *v.* FCC, 982 F.2d 1043 (7th Cir. 1992) (Posner, J.) (vacating and remanding financial interest and syndication rules to FCC as arbitrary and capricious).

24. 47 C.F.R. § 73.3555(d).

2. The MFJ, as mentioned earlier, imposes line-of-business restrictions that prevent the RBOCs from providing transmission service across LATA boundaries.

3. The tariffing process for common carriers slows the rate at which prices can be adjusted to respond to the pricing or entry actions of one's competitors.

4. The franchising process by which entrant common carriers must receive certificates of convenience and necessity impedes entry and can be used to make franchises exclusive even where natural monopoly characteristics are absent.

5. The protracted process by which the FCC allocates spectrum, and the inability of a licensee to redeploy its spectrum to a more highly valued use, act as a generic barrier to entry into any new wireless telecommunications service that threatens to compete with wireline services.[25]

These peculiar regulatory practices reduce the likelihood of obtaining the demand elasticities needed by Ramsey analysis to enable it to calculate correct second-best optimal prices in the telecommunications industry.

The Perfectly Contestable Market

The second alternative to use of the perfect-competition model as a guide for regulation rests on an equally theoretical concept, the hypothetical state of affairs called the *perfectly contestable market*. A market is said to be perfectly contestable if entry and exit are perfectly easy and costless—that is, if a competitor can enter without

---

25. The decade-long delay in allocating spectrum for mobile cellular telephony is estimated to have cost at least $86 billion in lost consumer welfare. *See* JEFFERY ROHLFS, CHARLES JACKSON & TRACEY KELLY, ESTIMATE OF THE LOSS TO THE UNITED STATES CAUSED BY THE FCC'S DELAY IN LICENSING CELLULAR TELECOMMUNICATIONS (National Economic Research Associates, Inc. Nov. 1991).

incurring any costs to which incumbents are not subject. Entry must not require the new firm to make any sunk investments—that is, to make outlays that cannot be quickly and costlessly retrieved. For where such outlays are required, entry becomes risky and hence costly, and exit certainly becomes expensive.

For a market to be perfectly contestable it is not necessary for instantaneous entry to be possible. Instead, the same consequences can be achieved by contracts between the entrant and the incumbent's former customers. Such contracts can protect the customers from exploitation by an incumbent supplier and can shield the entrant from retaliation by the incumbent by means such as predatory prices, giving the former all the time needed to enter the market.

A perfectly contestable market is a fictional ideal, no more to be found in reality than a market that is perfectly competitive. But, as noted before, the object of using this concept is to give regulators a model for the design of rules for markets that are distinctly *not* contestable. Perfect contestability is a generalization of perfect competition, since both require the complete absence of barriers to entry—that is, the absence of any costs that must be borne by an entrant but not by an incumbent. From the definition, it is clear that a market can be contestable whether or not its firms are large, and whether or not it is characterized by scale economies. Thus the concept escapes the impediments to applicability to regulatory issues that are the shortcomings of perfect competition in this arena. Yet a perfectly contestable market can serve as a model for regulation, because it offers all the guarantees of socially beneficial performance that perfect competition brings. In particular, perfect contestability ensures the following:

- Perfectly contestable markets permit the firm to earn the same profits it can obtain in a perfectly competitive market, and no more. Any earnings that exceed the cost of capital will attract new entrants, who can undercut the incumbent firm's prices and take its customers away.

- Perfectly contestable markets exclude any firm that is inefficient, because inefficiency enables efficient entrants to take the business away.

- Cross-subsidy cannot endure in a perfectly contestable market. That is, in a multiproduct firm, each product X must earn revenue at least sufficient to cover the increment in the firm's total cost that results from providing that service. This is so because no other product Y of the firm can provide excess profit with which to offset any losses incurred in the production of X, for the reasons just noted. Each product must fully pay its own way if the firm is to avoid insolvency.

- In a perfectly contestable market, as in a perfectly competitive one, the prices that prevail will be those required for economic efficiency and Pareto optimality. Since the reasoning underlying this last proposition is comparatively complicated, no attempt will be made here to summarize it.[26]

These four attributes indicate why the theoretical concept of a perfectly contestable market is qualified to serve as a competitive-market standard to guide regulation. Because perfect contestability does not require returns to scale to be either constant or diminishing, and because it does not preclude organization of an industry into a small number of large firms if that is more efficient than a multiplicity of minuscule enterprises, this competitive standard is sufficiently flexible to apply to telecommunications and a variety of other regulated industries. As a result, several regulatory agencies have adopted this competitive structure, at least one (the Interstate Commerce Commission) having done so explicitly in a major decision, and others having done so implicitly.[27]

---

26. For the full analysis that yields this result, as well as the qualifications required to report it accurately, see BAUMOL, PANZAR & WILLIG, *supra* note 13, at 24–29 (prop. 2b), 317–18 (prop. 11B5).

27. The ICC's seminal decisions are *Ex Parte* No. 347 (Sub-No.1), Coal Rate Guidelines—Nationwide (unpublished decision issued Feb. 8, 1983); Coal Rate Guidelines, Nationwide, 1 I.C.C.2d 520 (1985).

As we next turn to the specific regulatory issues facing local telephony, this practical consideration should be kept in mind. The regulatory principles under discussion in this arena, which seem to be gaining adherents among regulatory agencies, can be derived directly from contestable-markets analysis, even though they often deviate from the requirements of perfect competition.

Other Models for Optimal Regulation

It is sometimes said that the theory of contestable markets is a controversial subject. But that is not really so. There is considerable question, for example, about the frequency with which highly but imperfectly contestable markets are to be found in reality. Everyone agrees nonetheless that this frequency can only be determined by empirical research.

A different criticism sometimes directed at the competitive-market model is that it fails to incorporate the results in recent theoretical literature on regulation. This body of research makes impressive use of game theory and the theory of principal-agent relationships to construct models of the behavior of firms (and regulators) in settings in which regulators are constrained by limited information.[28] The regulator's assumed objective need not be the scrupulous pursuit of "the public interest, convenience, and necessity."

We have not attempted to survey this literature because it exceeds the scope of the present monograph. The recent theoretical literature on optimal regulation is still highly mathematical and abstract. Our purpose in this monograph, in contrast, is to describe in nontechnical terms the theoretical basis for reforms that regulators have undertaken, or are soon likely to undertake, in markets characterized by economies of scale and scope. Our omission should not be taken to denigrate the recent theoretical work. On the contrary, the insights from this research are likely in the future to improve the

---

28. *See* JEAN-JACQUES LAFFONT & JEAN TIROLE, A THEORY OF INCENTIVES IN PROCUREMENT AND REGULATION (MIT Press 1993); DANIEL F. SPULBER, REGULATION AND MARKETS (MIT Press 1989). For a less mathematical treatment of these subjects, see TRAIN, *supra* note 11.

recommendations fashioned here from the more familiar tools of price theory.

Conclusion

In this chapter we have explained the concepts of economic efficiency and Pareto optimality. These first principles support use of the competitive-market model as the appropriate standard for economic regulation. But the relevant notion of competition for that model is perfect contestability rather than perfect competition. For the latter assumes that a multiplicity of minuscule firms will populate a market—a state of affairs fundamentally inconsistent with the observed presence of economies of scale and scope in many regulated arenas. More important, the prescription for marginal-cost pricing that flows from the equilibrium conditions of a perfectly competitive market will ensure the bankruptcy of firms subject to scale economies.

Ramsey pricing is one alternative to the first-best solution of marginal-cost pricing. For a multiproduct firm, Ramsey analysis calls, in the least complex cases, for prices that deviate from marginal costs in inverse relationship to each product's price elasticity of demand. In this way, the firm can earn revenues sufficient to cover its total costs while keeping the resulting distortion of consumer choices and the loss of economic efficiency to a minimum. The difficulty of actually carrying out Ramsey pricing, however, has led regulators to learn from contestability analysis, and to embrace a different set of pricing rules, to which our discussion now turns.

Appendix 3–1: Formal Derivation of the Inverse-Elasticity Formula

Formal derivation of the inverse-elasticity formula is straightforward. For simplicity, the derivation that follows deals with a trivial economy containing only a single consumer and utilizing only a single input—labor. The result, however, is readily generalized. Here we let

y_i = the output of good i ($i = 1,..., n$)

$L* = $ the available quantity of labor time

$l* = $ unused labor time (leisure)

$p_i = $ the price of good i

$w = $ the wage rate (the price of leisure)

$U(y_1,\ldots, y_n, l*) = $ the consumer's utility function

$L(y_1,\ldots, y_n) = $ the quantity of labor required to product the vector of outputs

$MC_i = w\partial L/\partial y_i = $ the marginal cost of i

$MR_i = \partial \Sigma p_j y_j/\partial y_i = $ the marginal revenue of i

$E_i = $ the price elasticity of demand for good i.

Then the analysis seeks to

maximize $U(.)$, $\hfill$ (3.1)

subject to the resource availability constraint

$L(.) + l* = L*$ $\hfill$ (3.2)

and the financial breakeven constraint

$\Sigma p_i y_i = wL(.)$. $\hfill$ (3.3)

Using subscripts to denote partial differentiation (so that $U_i = \partial U/\partial y_i$), the Lagrangian expression is

$U(.) + \alpha[L* - l* - L(.)] + \beta[\Sigma p_i y_i - Wl(.)]$, $\hfill$ (3.4)

which yields the first-order conditions

$U_i - \alpha L_i = \beta(MR_i - MC_i)$ $\hfill$ (3.5)

$U_{l*} = \alpha$. $\hfill$ (3.6)

But equilibrium of the consumer requires proportionality between prices and marginal utilities, so that for some constant, k,

$U_i = kp_i, \; U_{l*} = kw$. $\hfill$ (3.7)

Thus, substituting Equation (3.7) into Equation (3.6), we get

$w = \alpha/k$, $\hfill$ (3.8)

and, substituting Equation (3.7) and Equation (3.8) into Equation (3.5), we have

$p_i - Wl_i = p_i - MC_i = (\beta/k)(MR_i - MC_i)$. $\hfill$ (3.9)

Where goods are neither substitutes nor complements, the standard formula $MR_i = p_i (1 - 1/E_i)$ holds. That formula, when substituted into Equation (3.9), yields

$$p_i - MC_i = (\beta/k)(p_i - MC_i - p_i/E_i) \tag{3.10}$$

or

$$(1 - \beta/k)(p_i - MC_i) = - (\beta/k)p_i/E_i, \tag{3.11}$$

that is,

$$(p_i - MC_i)/p_i = \delta/E_i, \tag{3.12}$$

for some constant δ independent of i, which is the inverse-elasticity formula.

4

Regulating the Pricing of
Final Products: Preliminary Concepts

FOR CONVENIENCE, the appropriate rules for public-interest price regulation will be divided in this monograph into two major topics: the pricing of final products, which is the subject of most immediate interest to final consumers of telecommunications services, and the pricing of such intermediate inputs as access to the local loop, a subject that most directly affects the supplier firms. The two topics will be explored in turn.

The logic and substance of the rules appropriate for the two subfields may appear to be different, but the differences are superficial. The two branches of the discussion are parts of a unified analysis in two senses. First, both constitute special applications of the same general principles. Second, the beneficial consequences of adopting one of the two sets of rules discussed in the chapters that follow will be greatly attenuated if the other set is substantially violated. If the supplier is permitted to price final products as an unregulated monopolist, for example, then the benefits of adopting the rules for access pricing will be reduced severely.

This chapter and the next two will focus on the determination of regulatory rules for final product prices. Intermediate-good prices are left to Chapter 7.

The Joint Role of Cost and Demand in Optimal Pricing of Final Products: The Floor-Ceiling Solution

One clear implication of Ramsey analysis is that where economies or diseconomies of scale are present, both the state of demand and the structure of costs *must* be taken into account in the setting of efficient prices. Only where constant returns to scale prevail in the neighborhood of the optimal combination of output levels for the set of services supplied by the industry do costs alone appear to determine optimal prices. Even there, where the familiar formula requires the price of each service to equal its marginal cost—a result also produced by the Ramsey formulas in the case of constant returns—the absence of demand considerations is deceptive. For marginal costs generally vary with the scale of output, and the scale of output cannot be determined without considering demand. Perhaps this special case of constant returns to scale may be interpreted as the erroneous justification for the traditional attempt by regulators to use costs alone as their standard for price setting.

Probably more to the point is the difficulty of obtaining and keeping current a comprehensive and reliable set of estimates of the pertinent demand relationships. Regulators generally understand that this task is beyond reasonable hope. We have noted that this difficulty is the key impediment to a regulatory regime that aspires to calculate and update a set of current Ramsey prices, which the regulated firms would be required to adopt. We do not know how to determine all the necessary own-price and cross-price elasticities, much less how to execute the constant updating needed to correct for obsolescence.

This data requirement is the prime regulatory dilemma besetting the pursuit of pricing rules that can elicit perfect economic efficiency. Current demand elasticities and other pertinent attributes of the demand relationships are virtually unobtainable in practice. Yet any prices calculated without the use of such information are apt to be inconsistent with economic efficiency, and are all too likely to damage economic welfare, rather than to help it. The solution toward which regulation of telecommunications and of other industries has moved, and the solution recommended by most economists engaged in the formulation of regulatory practice, is to divide the task into two parts. The first consists of imposing constraints upon the setting of prices by the firm—constraints derived from the competitive-market model just described, and which, fortunately, can be expressed in the required quantitative terms with the aid of cost information alone. The second part of the price-determination process is then left to management in the regulated firm, whose self-interest will lead it to take demand conditions into account. The regulated firm is prohibited from selecting any prices that violate the cost-based constraints adopted by the regulator; but within those limits the firm is granted the freedom to select the prices that best promote its interests.

More specifically, this regulatory approach proceeds, in effect, by setting a ceiling over every price, as well as a floor below which the price is not permitted to go. This ceiling and floor are derived from the competitive-market model directly. Thus, the firm is never permitted to adopt a price so high that it could not prevail in a perfectly contestable market, but it is allowed to set a price at any level that could prevail in the long run in such a market. The price floors are derived in a similar manner. The particulars of this derivation and the nature of the floors and ceilings that emerge will be described below. For the moment, however, this brief description is sufficient to suggest the spirit of the approach. In essence, it seeks to enforce competitive behavior in arenas where such behavior is not the automatic result of market conditions.

Little need be lost even when regulators adopt such a floor and ceiling and calculate their magnitudes correctly but do so in the erroneous belief that the market is insufficiently competitive. For if the market actually is highly competitive, although not recognized as such, the regulator merely will ensure that the firm behaves as the pressures of competition already force it to do. Of course, the serious danger remains that a regulatory error in evaluating the competitiveness of the market will be compounded by a miscalculation of the floor and ceiling. Then, the costs to society can be great. But this risk of miscalculation by regulators is not unique to a regulatory regime built on the theory of perfect contestability; rather, it besets every form of price regulation.

The primary purpose of the price ceiling, aside from its role in eliciting economic efficiency, is to protect consumers—both household and business purchasers of telecommunications services—from monopolistic exploitation through the imposition of excessive prices by the regulated firm. Similarly, the primary purpose of the price floors, economic efficiency aside, is to protect actual or prospective rivals of the regulated firm from predatory pricing and related practices that can seriously handicap these competitors in the competitive process or drive them from the field altogether.

Business Self-Interest and Public-Interest Pricing

Why should the management of the regulated firm, given freedom to adapt its prices to demand conditions in whatever way it chooses within the constraints imposed by the regulatory floor and ceiling, voluntarily always select prices that serve the public interest? This proposition surely cannot be accepted as an article of faith. There is some reason, however, to conclude that self-interest indeed will lead to an approximation of public-interest pricing in these circumstances. To see why this is so, we must return to Ramsey analysis, demonstrating once more the valuable role it can play as a general guide, even though it is unusable for selecting individual prices.

The Ramsey rules call for differentiated prices. The inverse-elasticity rule, or the more complex counterpart rules of more general applicability, indeed can be interpreted as public-interest recipes for the systematic deviation of prices from marginal costs. It is well known in economic theory that the profit-maximizing firm, if it can adopt differential prices, will find it most profitable to select prices that deviate from marginal costs inversely with the respective price elasticities of demand. This holds true where the various goods are neither substitutes nor complements.[1] Indeed, where the cross-price elasticities of demand for some or all of the firm's products are not zero, profitability will be served by also taking these elasticities into account in the manner that the generalized Ramsey formula prescribes. This is what defenders of the practice have dubbed "value-of-service

---

1. *See, e.g.,* JEAN TIROLE, THE THEORY OF INDUSTRIAL ORGANIZATION 66, 137 (MIT Press 1988).

pricing," while its critics have referred to it as "charging what the traffic will bear." This discussion invites the cynic to remark that in the final analysis, the Ramsey rules are no more than a rationalization for the practices of price-discriminating monopolists.[2]

But monopoly prices will generally be very different from Ramsey prices. Prices that follow the Ramsey rule are constrained to yield profits no higher than the competitive earnings level, while the discriminating monopolist's profits are unconstrained. It is easy to show that prices in the presence of a profit constraint differ from those adopted when such a constraint is absent. The former are generally far lower than the latter. Moreover, while the former of these sets of prices produces economic efficiency, as Ramsey analysis demonstrates, the latter can be expected to damage the public interest, perhaps severely.

In any event, the regulated firm, permitted to select any prices it desires, subject to the floor and ceiling constraints, has as much incentive as the unregulated, price-discriminating firm to respond to demand elasticities in the manner just described. The regulated firm, permitted to earn competitive profits, may fail to earn even these if it does not take demand conditions into account in selecting its prices. Business management is well aware that it can be suicidal to raise prices predominantly on items whose demand is elastic.

Theoretically, this argument is not conclusive. There will generally be a continuum of price vectors, all of which are capable of yielding exactly zero economic profits. The set of these prices is, for example, a staple of the Averch-Johnson literature that discusses the distorting influence of rate-of-return regulation on the input proportions selected by the firm.[3] But in practice, uncertainty is the hallmark of price setting, and no real-world business management knows the range of price vectors that will yield exactly the profits that regulation permits. It generally is happy to have any confidence that a particular price

---

2. For a representative denunciation of Ramsey pricing as price gouging, see the initial decision of the administrative law judge in American Tel. & Tel. Co., Dkt. No. 19129, 64 F.C.C.2d 131, 469–70 ¶¶ 1121–24 (1976).

3. *See* Harvey Averch & Leland L. Johnson, *Behavior of the Firm under Regulatory Constraint,* 52 AM. ECON. REV. 1053 (1962).

vector it can identify is capable of doing the job. In these circumstances, management can surely be relied upon to resist raising the prices of items with elastic demands and holding down the prices of items whose demands are believed to be inelastic.[4]

Although the demand information available to management is highly imperfect, it seems likely that management will have a better and more up-to-date estimate of demand conditions than the regulator, who is so much further removed from the marketing firing line. In short, the firm can generally be taken to have superior information about demand and to have some considerable incentive to adapt its prices to demand conditions in roughly the manner that best serves the public interest. In this imperfect world, with its persistently incomplete and inaccurate demand information, this is probably the best that can be hoped for.

The Meaning and Enforcement of Competitive-Profit Ceilings

The preceding discussion insinuated a premise that may appear unwarranted: that the regulated firm is permitted to earn no more than competitive profits. The attempt to enforce such a rule was a hallmark of rate-base rate-of-return regulation, which is now widely discredited both because it discourages efficiency and productivity growth and because it leads to perpetual litigation. By denying the regulated firm any possibility of superior reward for superior efficiency or productivity performance, this approach has led to technological stagnation in some regulatory arenas and has impeded progress in others. We consequently reject a return to this approach as a possibility that merits consideration.

Where, then, does any ceiling on *earnings* enter the matter? As will be explained, it is introduced through the *price* ceilings that the competitive-market model entails. Clearly, sufficiently severe ceilings on prices can restrict profits to any degree desired. In regulation that follows the competitive-market model, however, the relation is far more subtle, as will be shown later. Here, it is enough to note that this

---

4. For a more theoretical argument indicating another source of incentive for management to adopt Ramsey pricing, see William J. Baumol, Elizabeth E. Bailey & Robert D. Willig, *Weak Invisible Hand Theorems on the Sustainability of Multiproduct Natural Monopoly*, 67 AM. ECON. REV. 350 (1977).

desideratum is addressed in the regulatory rules that follow the competitive-market guidelines. It is useful, however, to note three important caveats:

1. No one figure can be taken to constitute the "proper" universal value for the current competitive rate of return. Risk must be taken into account in determining such a figure for a particular industry, with the competitive rate of return set higher the riskier the industry in question. The reasons should be obvious.

2. Competitive industries can expect to earn a return equal to their cost of capital (zero economic profit), but they can be expected to do so only on the average and in the long run. It does not violate the rules of even perfect competition that a firm which loses money during a recession recoups those losses through earnings that temporarily exceed the cost of capital during an ensuing period of prosperity.

3. Even in competitive markets, firms with superior innovation and productivity growth can expect as their reward earnings temporarily exceeding the cost of capital. That is the incentive for the firm to undertake the effort and risk entailed in the innovation process.

In short, regulation that undertakes to follow the competitive-market model and to prevent excess profits must not adopt rules that prohibit any of these three forms of deviation from zero economic profits, lest the result damage the public interest.

The Pertinent Cost Concepts

The form of market-guided regulation under discussion here operates via floors and ceilings upon prices in those arenas where the power of competition is deemed to be insufficient. Those floors and ceilings, in turn, are based upon costs. The five recurring cost concepts include fully distributed cost (or fully allocated cost), marginal cost, incremental cost, average-incremental cost, and stand-alone cost. They are defined as follows:

Fully Distributed Cost (FDC). This traditional tool of price regulation is now generally discredited and is increasingly being abandoned in regulatory practice. The fully distributed cost of product X is defined as the outlay per unit of output of X, including all expenses clearly attributable to X alone, plus some share of any common costs incurred on behalf of X and one or more other outputs. Since it is generally impossible to determine "the" proportion of such common costs that should be attributed to X, the division of common costs among the various outputs on whose behalf they are incurred is always carried out on the basis of an admittedly arbitrary rule of thumb, usually designed by accounting practice. Fully distributed cost is defined so that the sum of the fully distributed costs of the various outputs of the firm equals the total cost of the enterprise. Usually, the choice of an arbitrary rule for apportioning common costs profoundly affects the magnitudes of the individual FDC figures that emerge from the calculation. Not surprisingly, therefore, the selection made among alternative rules has sparked bitter and protracted disputes between parties seeking to impose low floors and those favoring high floors for the prices of particular regulated commodities. In any event, since the FDC figures are arbitrary, only by very unlikely happenstance will the numbers that emerge from any particular FDC calculation have any relation to the prices required for economic efficiency.[5]

Marginal Cost of X. This concept refers to the increase in the firm's total outlays resulting from a small rise in the output of X. As already noted, in perfectly competitive equilibrium the firm will always set the price of X equal to the marginal cost of X, and this price will satisfy the requirements of economic efficiency if it yields revenue sufficient for continued financial solvency of the firm. But

---

5. For more on the problems engendered by using fully distributed cost, see William J. Baumol, Michael F. Koehn & Robert D. Willig, *How Arbitrary Is "Arbitrary"?—or, Toward the Deserved Demise of Full Cost Allocation*, PUB. UTIL. FORTNIGHTLY, vol. 120, no. 5, at 16 (Sept. 3, 1987).

such a price will always prevent the earning of revenues sufficient for this purpose where production is characterized by scale economies.

Incremental Cost of X. Incremental cost is a generic concept referring to the addition, per unit of the additional output in question, to the firm's total cost when the output of X expands by some preselected increment. Thus, marginal cost can be approximated by incremental cost if the increment in question is small. But if the increment is large, marginal cost and incremental cost can differ substantially, because the ranges of outputs examined in the two calculations are not the same.

Average-Incremental Cost for an Entire Service X (AIC_X). Average-incremental cost, along with marginal cost, is the concept most frequently cited in recent discussions of public-interest floors on prices. The average-incremental cost of the entire service is defined as the difference in the firm's total costs with and without service X supplied, divided by the output of X. In other words, it is the cost per unit of X that is added to the firm's total outlays as a result of its supply of the current output of X. Formally, if we let $x, y, z, \ldots$ represent the outputs of the firm's various products, and $TC(x, y, z, \ldots)$ is the total amount the firm must expend in producing that combination of outputs, then we have

$$AIC_X = [TC(x, y, z, \ldots) - TC(0, y, z, \ldots)]/x.$$

It is natural to consider average-incremental cost as a first cousin of the commonly used *average-variable cost.* Because, so far as we are aware, there is no standard definition of the latter, the difference between or similarity of the two concepts cannot be determined conclusively. They *can* be used to mean the same thing, but there are at least three differences in the ways they are often interpreted or utilized.

First, average-variable cost is used at least sometimes to refer to short-run cost, with capacity not adjusted to output volume, while average-incremental cost is the lower, long-run figure obtained after plant and equipment are adjusted so as to minimize the average cost of the pertinent output. Second, average-incremental cost of a service *X* includes any fixed cost that must be incurred on behalf of that product alone. In private correspondence with one of the present authors, Professor Phillip Areeda has indicated that his definition of average-variable cost, which is used extensively in antitrust litigation,[6] *does* include such "product-specific" fixed costs.[7] But it is not clear that this is done by everyone who calculates average-variable-cost figures. Finally, average-variable-cost calculations are burdened by the baggage of past calculation practices of questionable legitimacy, from which average-incremental-cost studies so far seem to be freer.

Despite these three possible differences, readers will lose little in following the logic in the remainder of our discussion if they treat average-incremental cost and average-variable cost as synonyms.

Stand-Alone Cost of a Combination of Services Y,Z,... ($SAC_{Y,Z,...}$). This is the cost that would be incurred by an efficient entrant to the industry in question if it were to decide to produce only some specified set of commodities *Y,Z,....* That is, it is the cost to produce just those items, "standing alone." The concept also applies to an entrant that decides to produce only a single commodity *Y.* Using the preceding notation, we can write, for the case where the entrant decides to produce *Y,Z,...* but not *X,*

$$SAC_{Y,Z,...} = TC(0, y, z, ...).$$

Under the competitive-market standard for regulation, marginal costs and average-incremental costs are the figures pertinent for price floors, while stand-alone costs are the costs relevant for price ceilings. Moreover, as we will show in Chapter 6, incremental cost and stand-alone cost are intimately connected, and either number can be deduced directly from the other. Specifically, when the firm earns no more and

6. Phillip Areeda & Donald F. Turner, *Predatory Pricing and Related Practices Under Section 2 of the Sherman Act*, 88 HARV. L. REV. 697 (1975).

7. *See* WILLIAM J. BAUMOL, SUPERFAIRNESS: APPLICATIONS AND THEORY 116 n.4, 118 n.6 (MIT Press 1986).

no less than the competitive rate of return, if each of the firm's prices is above its average-incremental cost, then each of those prices *must* be below its stand-alone cost, and vice versa. This result can simplify the administration of price floors and ceilings.

Cost of Capital, Opportunity Cost, and Replacement Cost

Three observations are pertinent to the calculation of marginal cost, average-incremental cost, or stand-alone cost. First, any of these three cost figures must include the cost of capital, which obviously must be covered if the regulated firm is to be able to continue in operation. The amount of capital in question, however, is determined differently for each cost concept. In calculating the average-incremental cost of X, for example, one must consider the increment in the firm's capital necessitated by the decision to produce X.

Second, any of these cost figures always must include the pertinent opportunity costs—that is, earnings from alternative sources that the firm forgoes by undertaking the action in question. Suppose, for example, that the firm's owners undertake to produce product X and, as part of this undertaking, invest $5 million in the enterprise. Suppose further that government bonds currently pay 9 percent interest and that such bonds are the best alternative investment available. The firm's investment decision, then, causes the owners to forgo $450,000 in interest each year—that is, 9 percent of $5 million—that they could have earned by investing their money in bonds rather than in expanding the firm's activities. This $450,000 is the annual opportunity cost of the incremental capital they invest to introduce product X, and it is a real component of the cost of capital. For if the firm's earnings cannot be expected to cover this forgone income, the investors will not supply the $5 million to the firm—just as a bank would be unwilling to lend the money under similar circumstances. In equilibrium in a perfectly competitive or contestable market, the firm's revenues will always cover opportunity cost. Moreover, this condition is required for economic efficiency. That is, it is required to attract capital to those uses where it makes the greatest contribution to output—uses where the available earnings at least equal the earnings that could have been obtained by devoting that capital to the second-best investment opportunity.

Third, where the firm uses assets purchased in the past, the cost of using them also must be evaluated as the opportunity cost of that use—that is, the price that those assets could fetch if transferred to an alternative use. In a business where demand is sufficient to make it profitable to replace those assets at the appropriate time, the assets will be valued in a competitive market at the current cost of the most economical replacement of the remaining output capacity of those old assets. No buyer will pay any more than this replacement cost for those assets, and their current owner will be unwilling to sell such profitable assets for any less.

Conclusion

This concludes our exposition of the basic concepts from which to fashion regulatory rules for pricing final outputs. We have explained the role of demand in efficient pricing, as indicated by Ramsey analysis. We have also defined the pertinent cost concepts—average-incremental cost and stand-alone cost—from which price floors and ceilings can be calculated to simulate equilibrium requirements in a perfectly contestable market. We will next show how these price floors and ceilings promote economic efficiency in the market for final products in local telephone service.

5

Price Floors for Final Products

ON FIRST CONSIDERATION it may seem that the public interest hardly justifies the imposition of any floors on prices—the lower the better for consumers. But more careful deliberation indicates that this is not so. Indeed, economic analysis confirms that an excessively low price can be as damaging to economic efficiency as an excessively high one. An excessively low price is an incentive to overuse resources and to ignore waste in their employment. Economic analysis of public-interest pricing thus indicates that a firm with market power should be restrained from adopting, for presumably illegitimate competitive purposes, too low a price, just as it is restrained from adopting one that is excessive.

Additional reasons of greater urgency also call for price floors. Prices that are too low may come at the expense of adequacy of investment, preventing expansion of capacity, modernization of facilities, and ultimately, continued operation of the supplier firms. It may sometimes even be appropriate to prevent competing firms from driving one another into suicide by adoption of uncompensatory prices through price wars or other related forms of behavior.

Cross-Subsidy and Predatory Pricing Defined

Much more likely, however, is the possibility that excessively low prices, perhaps financed by cross-subsidy, can be used for predatory purposes. The terms "cross-subsidy" and "predatory pricing," until recently rather vague, have now acquired clear meanings based in part on economic theory. Because they recur in regulatory proceedings, including those concerned with local telephone service, it is useful to discuss their connotations briefly.

A *cross-subsidy* is present when the average-incremental revenue contributed by a product of a firm is insufficient to cover its average-incremental cost, but the firm nevertheless earns sufficient revenue from all its products to cover its cost of capital together with its other outlays. For if this is so, some other products of the firm must be priced sufficiently high to bring in the revenue required to offset the shortfall of the revenues of the cross-subsidized product. Thus, one can say that a service X receives a subsidy if its revenues are inadequate to cover the costs caused by the firm's supply of X, but the firm's operations are financially viable nevertheless. The test of a cross-subsidy most usually compares the (fixed) price of service X (which equals its average-incremental revenue) with its average-incremental cost. If the firm never sells at a price lower than that cost, it is adjudged not to be receiving a cross-subsidy.

The definition of cross-subsidy is sometimes expressed in terms of *gross* incremental revenues and costs, and sometimes in terms of the *net* figures.[1] This is not the place to review the arguments that have been raised for and against either of these tests vis-á-vis the other. It is clear, however, that any calculation that uses net incremental revenue must also use net incremental cost, and that any calculation that uses gross figures must also use them consistently for both revenues and costs.

---

1. The net incremental revenue of a service X is the revenue contributed by X minus any loss (plus any gain) in revenue from any other service Y that results because the supply of X reduces (increases) sales of Y. Net cost is defined correspondingly. Gross incremental revenue and costs are the figures that have not been adjusted for any such cross-elasticities of demand. In regulatory practice, the term "incremental-cost test" usually refers to the comparison of gross incremental revenues and costs, while the corresponding comparison of the net figure is usually called the "burden test," because any service whose net incremental revenues at least cover its net incremental costs is said to impose no financial burden on the purchasers of other products of the same firm. *See* WILLIAM J. BAUMOL, SUPERFAIRNESS: APPLICATIONS AND THEORY 115–20 (MIT Press 1986).

A price is *predatory* if it is so low that all three of the following are true: (1) the price will reduce the long-run earnings of the firm unless it succeeds in eliminating or reducing competition; (2) the price can drive other firms out of business or prevent the entry of efficient rivals; and (3) after the exit of competitors or the prevention of entry, it can be expected that it will be possible to raise the price sufficiently above the competitive level and for a sufficient time to recoup the earlier profit sacrifice and more. In sum, the price in question is predatory only if it has no legitimate business reason and its profitability is entirely contingent on eliminating rivals.

Our economic definition of predatory pricing comports with the legal test enunciated by the Supreme Court in its 1993 decision in *Brooke Group Ltd. v. Brown & Williamson Tobacco Corp.*[2] A showing of predatory pricing requires that the plaintiff prove (1) "that the prices complained of are below an appropriate measure of its rival's costs," and (2) "that the competitor had a reasonable prospect, or . . . a dangerous probability, of recouping its investment in below-cost prices."[3] Elaborating on the second element of this test, the Court said that "[f]or recoupment to occur, below-cost pricing must be capable, as a threshold matter, of producing the intended effects on the firm's rivals," such as "driving them from the market."[4] Although the three conditions in our economic definition of predatory pricing do not expressly mention "pricing below cost," the relevance of cost floors to that definition, and thus the compatibility of our definition with the *Brown & Williamson* test, will become clear presently.

Both cross-subsidy and predation can be legitimate fears of competitors of the regulated firm—although, in the absence of rate-base rate-of-return regulation, the danger may be no greater than when the competitor is unregulated. And, obviously, both phenomena threaten the interest of consumers in the continued vigor of competition. Both cross-subsidy and predatory pricing, by their very nature, can be pre-

2. Brooke Group Ltd. *v.* Brown & Williamson Tobacco Corp., 113 S. Ct. 2578 (1993). The opposing lawyers in oral argument before the Supreme Court were two antitrust scholars, Professor Phillip Areeda and Judge Robert Bork.

3. *Id.* at 2587-88. Significantly, the Court noted: "Because the parties in this case agree that the relevant measure of cost is average variable cost, . . . we again decline to resolve the conflict . . . over the appropriate measure of cost." *Id.* at 2587 n.1.

4. *Id.* at 2589.

vented by adopting suitable floors under prices. Thus the imposition of floors under the prices of the regulated firm suspected of possessing market power is not merely a way for one firm to protect itself from excessively vigorous price competition by another, although price floors arguably have often been advocated for that self-interested purpose. Price floors also have a legitimate justification as instruments for promoting the public interest. But to play that role well, the price-floor figure must be selected with care and founded upon the logic of the competitive-market model.

Marginal Cost as a Legitimate Floor

As economists all recognize, no firm in a competitive market will for any substantial time offer any product at a price below its marginal cost. For if it were to do so, the firm could increase its profit by reducing its output of the product. In other words, the price in that case is by definition not covering the cost incurred by the last increment in the firm's production of the item. The only rational purpose that the firm can have in continuing to supply its current output of that product at such a price is predation.

In a perfectly competitive or perfectly contestable market, however, predation can never succeed. The costlessness of entry and exit ensures that the firm with predatory intentions can never earn the monopoly profits that are the ultimate objective of using initially low prices to drive rivals from the field. Thus, in such markets price will never fall below marginal cost, except perhaps through a temporary error or for some other equally transitory reason. This means that the competitive-market model immediately leads to adoption of marginal cost (or of a demonstrably approximating average-incremental-cost figure, if that is easier to calculate in practice) as a legitimate regulatory floor under prices.

It is also easy to see that price should be kept from falling below marginal cost, lest economic efficiency be harmed. Suppose that firm *A* can produce a portion of market output more efficiently than *B*, meaning that the marginal cost of this output is lower for *A* than for *B*. If *B* nevertheless is able to price below marginal cost, it may well get the business in question, even though the cost to the economy caused by having the marginal sales go to *B* are higher than if these units of product had been supplied by *A*.

Thus we conclude that marginal cost is a legitimate floor under prices, one prescribed by the competitive-market model and the requirements of economic efficiency.

Average-Incremental Cost of the Entire Product as a Legitimate Price Floor

Marginal cost is not the only legitimate price floor, however. The average-incremental cost of the entire product has an equally defensible claim upon this role where the same price is charged to all buyers of the product in question—that is, where there is no differential pricing. The output over which the averaging occurs must be homogeneous, and the average refers to the average of the marginal cost of the first customer plus that of the second, and so forth. But it certainly is *not* legitimate for this purpose to average the costs of different products. If, for example, *A* lives next door to the home office of a newspaper delivery service, but *B* lives far out of town, and the cost of delivery to *B* is very high, it is clearly illegitimate to average the two costs and to claim that the price to *A* must exceed this average. For here the two customers receive different delivery services. Henceforth, unless otherwise specified, the shorter term average-incremental cost (AIC) will be used to refer to the average-incremental cost of the entire product.

The justifications for using average-incremental cost as the price floor are almost precisely the same as those for using marginal cost. This second standard, nevertheless, may be unfamiliar to economists who do not specialize in regulatory matters and whose training is largely in marginal analysis. In particular, the requirement that price not be below either marginal cost or AIC bears some resemblance to the Areeda-Turner test for predatory pricing, which requires price to exceed marginal cost, and which permits the use of average-variable cost instead of marginal cost when it is difficult to calculate the latter.[5] The

5. Phillip Areeda & Donald F. Turner, *Predatory Pricing and Related Practices Under*

two criteria are not the same, however. First, AIC includes "product-specific" fixed costs—that is, fixed costs incurred only on behalf of the product in question. As noted in Chapter 4, it is not clear that this is true of average-variable cost. Second, in the Areeda-Turner analysis, average-variable cost is not in itself an essential part of the cost floor. It is merely a quick and dirty way to calculate an approximation to marginal cost.

A little thought will confirm that no competitive firm will long supply any product at a fixed price that does not cover its average-incremental cost. The reason is the same as before. If X is the firm's only product, a uniform price that does not cover the average-incremental cost of X means that the firm must be losing money, and that condition cannot continue indefinitely. And if the firm supplies a multiplicity of products, it could increase its total profits either by raising the price of X above its AIC, or by discontinuing its supply of product X, whose revenues are less than the costs it causes. Thus, in the absence of differential pricing (with different units of a homogeneous product sold at different prices), predation is the only rational reason for a firm to supply X at a price below AIC. But in a fully competitive market, predation cannot succeed, as we have seen. Thus, the competitive-market model also shows the legitimacy of average-incremental cost as a price floor.

The same analysis as before also shows why this rule is required for economic efficiency when there is a choice between two or more firms as the suppliers of a given vector, or basket, of outputs. If firm A is the more efficient supplier of its share of the market for product X because A has the lower average-incremental cost at that output level, B may nevertheless be able to get the business away from A if B is permitted to adopt a uniform price below its average-incremental cost. If so, the result will be that more resources than the minimum necessary will be expended in bringing X to consumers, which clearly violates economic efficiency.

It should be noted, incidentally, that enforcement of the average-incremental-cost price floor guarantees that no cross-subsidy will occur, since, as we saw, the standard test tells us that a cross-subsidy is present only if price is less than AIC. That price floor can also be taken to preclude predatory pricing, because any product price that at least covers the product's average-incremental cost must by definition be contributing a profit, or at least incurring no loss.

The Combined Role of the Two Cost Floors

Although the preceding discussion may make it appear that there are two different cost standards, each jockeying for the position of regulatory cost floor, that is not so. In reality there can only be one such floor, the higher of the two figures in question. That is, if a uniform price is required to be higher than marginal cost and it is also required to be higher than average-incremental cost, it obviously must equal or exceed whichever of the two happens to be higher. The higher of the two figures becomes what we may refer to as the *effective price floor*. Which of the two happens to occupy that position, however, is not a fortuitous matter. Here we have the following general rule:

> If there are economies of scale in the sense that average-incremental cost falls lower and lower the larger the volume of output, then marginal cost must be below average-incremental cost, so that the latter must constitute the effective floor on prices. If average-incremental cost neither declines nor increases when output grows, then marginal cost and average-incremental cost must be equal, and either constitutes the effective price floor. Finally, if average-incremental cost rises when output increases, then marginal cost will always be the higher of the two, and it must therefore serve as the effective price floor.

The reason for this universally valid rule, a commonplace of elementary economic theory, is easily indicated by example.

Suppose that it costs $100 to produce one unit of X (the marginal cost of the first unit is $100), that the marginal cost of a second unit is $80, and that the marginal cost of a third unit is $30. Then, if three units of the product are actually sold, the total increment in the company's costs caused by the supply of X must equal $100 plus $80 plus $30, or $210. Hence, the average-incremental cost of the three units of output must equal $210 divided by 3, or $70. What we have seen so far is that average-incremental cost is, by definition, the average of the marginal costs of all the units of output supplied.

Now suppose that business expands and the firm decides to produce a fourth unit of X. Will the average-incremental cost of X rise above its previous level of $70, or will it fall below that number? The average will fall only if the new entry into the averaging calculation is below the old average, for only a below-average number can pull an average down. Thus, the AIC for four units of output will decline from its previous $70 level if the marginal cost of the fourth unit of X is less than $70. But if the marginal cost of the fourth unit of X exceeds $70, it will pull up the old average. If, for example, that marginal cost happens to be $71, the AIC will rise to $70.25—that is, ($100 + $80 + $30 + $71)/4, or $281/4.

Thus we conclude that in an industry where average-incremental cost declines when output increases, AIC must be greater than marginal cost, and AIC must be the effective price floor. If AIC moves in the opposite direction when output increases, marginal cost will be the effective floor. In local telephone service the evidence, though not conclusive, suggests that for many of the local services average-incremental cost declines, but so slowly when output increases that it is approximately constant. If so, average-incremental cost is the pertinent floor, but marginal cost is apt to constitute a fairly close approximation to average-incremental cost. That cannot simply be assumed, however. Anyone advocating the use of one floor rather than the other must provide the evidence required to justify that choice.

In a competitive market, prices will sometimes be set close to the floor. If demand conditions for service X are such, for example, that the profit-maximizing price barely exceeds average-incremental cost, the service will then make only a correspondingly low contribution to company profits. But some contribution is better than none, and in the absence of better alternatives it will pay to continue to offer X on these terms. The implication is clear: under the terms of the competitive-market model for regulation, it is the regulator's obligation to prevent any price of the regulated firm from being set below the floor just described.

Common Costs and Floors for Combinations of Services

We noted earlier that, by definition, marginal cost makes no contribution toward recovery of any fixed costs of the firm. A similar problem, only slightly modified, arises for average-incremental cost. This cost figure does include any fixed cost incurred exclusively for the service in question. But the average-incremental cost of service X does not include any contribution toward any fixed costs incurred *in common* for X and some other service or services supplied by the same firm. Suppose for example that supply of service X requires the construction of a specialized switching center that is of no help to any other service, and that such centers can be built only with rather substantial capacity. Over a broad range, the total cost of this switching center will consequently not rise when output of X increases, and so the cost in question is fixed and does not enter into the marginal cost of X. But, it is *incremental* to service X—that is, this outlay would never have been incurred if the company had decided not to supply X.

Next, suppose that equipment used to produce service X and equipment used to produce service Y are both housed in a single space that must be carefully air-conditioned to prevent contamination of the equipment. The outlay for air conditioning must be made if the company supplies only X, only Y, or both X and Y. Consequently, the cost of the air-conditioning equipment is not incremental to either X or Y alone. If either service were discontinued, the company could not avoid the cost of replacing the air conditioner when the time for that arrived. Nor can one argue that the air-conditioner cost is the responsibility of the service that happened to be provided first. That the company started to supply X in 1980, while Y was not introduced until 1987, is an irrelevant piece of history. Today, neither service can be provided without the air conditioning, and once the firm has decided to continue either one of the services, provision of the other adds zero to total air-conditioning costs. Thus the air conditioning is not part of the incremental cost of either X or Y; and since the cost is fixed, it is also not part of either service's marginal cost.

This difficulty in attributing cost has generated considerable concern over use of either marginal cost or average-incremental cost as a price floor. If a price that exceeds both includes no contribution to the firm's common fixed costs, how can that price be compensatory? Is the approach therefore not simply an invitation to below-cost pricing? The answer would be yes if what has been said so far were all there is to setting price floors on the competitive-market model. But there is more.

The next step in the full set of requirements that such a floor must satisfy is suggested by our air-conditioning example. We have seen that the air conditioner constitutes no part of the incremental cost of either X or Y by itself. *But it is distinctly included in the incremental cost of X and Y in combination.* Thus, to satisfy the proper test of price floors in this example, the following *three* conditions must *all* be satisfied: (1) the price of X must at least equal the AIC of X; (2) the price of Y must at least equal the AIC of Y; and (3) the prices of X and Y must be such that their combined incremental revenue at least equals the combined incremental cost of X and Y together. This is the combinatorial form of the incremental-cost test, first introduced by Professor Gerald Faulhaber.[6] A firm in a competitive market must price in a manner that satisfies the combinatorial price-floor test; otherwise, if its operation entails any appreciable common fixed costs, the firm will soon be out of business.

The combinatorial cost test is critically important for simplifying regulatory hearings and terminating the tedious and costly battles over the proper methods for full allocation of common fixed costs supposedly required to prevent cross-subsidy. The analysis underlying the combinatorial cost tests again emphasizes that such full allocations are impossible except by unavoidably arbitrary criteria, so that the results are inevitably without economic meaning. More important, the analysis shows that such allocation is unnecessary to prevent cross-subsidy, and that the combinatorial cost test can do the job satisfactorily.

The combinatorial test asserts, then, that the prices of the firm must be such that the resulting revenue of every product by itself, *and the combined revenue of every combination of the firm's products,* must at least equal the corresponding average-incremental cost. Anyone

6. Gerald R. Faulhaber, *Cross-Subsidization: Pricing in Public Enterprise*, 65 AM. ECON. REV. 966 (1975).

familiar with the algebra of combinations is apt to be taken aback by this requirement, because the number of combinations to be tested grows unmanageably as the number of the firm's products increases. A seven-product firm, for example, has 127 product combinations. But a ten-product firm has 1,023 product combinations, and a thirteen-product firm has 8,191.[7] In practice, however, because it is often possible to verify that many combinations of a firm's products entail no common fixed costs, the task is considerably simplified.

Consider, for example, the pertinent cost conditions for a hypothetical firm whose six products, denoted as *A* through *F*, have, for ease of exposition, a rather limited number of common costs. Each of the six products has its own average-incremental cost figure, and each product price must be compared with the corresponding AIC. Suppose that products *A* and *B* share a common cost C(*A,B*), so that their combined revenue R(*A*) + R(*B*) must equal or exceed their common cost C(*A,B*) plus the sum of their individual incremental costs. That is, we must have:

$$R(A) + R(B) \geq C(A,B) + \text{AIC}_A + \text{AIC}_B. \tag{5.1}$$

Next, suppose that products *B*, *C*, *D*, *E*, and *F* share a common cost, so that a test similar to the preceding one must be passed by these five products together:

$$R(B) + R(C) + R(D) + R(E) + R(F) \geq$$

---

7. For a firm producing *n* different products, the number of possible product combinations is

$$\sum_{r=1}^{n} \frac{n!}{r!(n-r)!}$$

See, e.g., 1 WILLIAM FELLER, AN INTRODUCTION TO PROBABILITY THEORY AND ITS APPLICATIONS 34 (John Wiley & Sons, Inc., 3d ed. 1968). That is, the total number of possible product combinations is the sum of *n* products taken one at a time, plus *n* products taken two at a time, plus *n* products taken three at a time, and so on, until *n* products are taken *n* at a time. Applying this summation of combinations to a seven-product firm shows that the total number of product combinations is 7 + 21 + 35 + 35 + 21 + 7 + 1 = 127.

$$C(B,C,D,E,F) + AIC_B + AIC_C + AIC_D + AIC_E + AIC_F. \quad (5.2)$$

Finally, it is crucial to note that the corresponding test must be passed by all six product lines together:

$$R(A) + R(B) + R(C) + R(D) + R(E) + R(F) \geq$$

$$C(A,B) + C(B,C,D,E,F) + C(A,B,C,D,E,F) +$$

$$AIC_A + AIC_B + AIC_C + AIC_D + AIC_E + AIC_F. \quad (5.3)$$

The common cost $C(A,B,C,D,E,F)$ is a fixed cost shared by all six of the firm's product lines—such as the cost of senior management in a large, diversified corporation. Since each cost figure is constructed to include the cost of capital, this last test is tantamount to the requirement that the company's total revenue from all its products must cover all the company's costs, including its cost of capital. This is equivalent to the requirement that the revenues be adequate for the continued financial solvency of the company.

Earlier, we stated that the procedures described here for executing the rules of the competitive-market model ensure that the firm's prices will be consistent with a competitive level of earnings. The combinatorial cost test is the first half of the calculations that ensure this result. It guarantees that unless market conditions prevent it (as when evolving consumer tastes make the firm's products obsolete), the firm will be constrained in a manner that provides revenues adequate for its continued operations. We will see in Chapter 6 that the price-ceiling rules complete the story and prevent those earnings from exceeding competitive levels, without eliminating the incentives for innovation and productivity growth.

Price Floors and Services Offered Under Contract

A pricing problem likely to become a substantial source of conflict under liberalized regulation arises when a supplier of telecommunications services contracts with a large customer to supply services on special terms arranged just with that customer.[8] It is clear that this is an opportunity for differential pricing—or, in the economist's terms, price discrimination. As is well known, even though price discrimination entails sales to one customer at a lower price relative to marginal cost than the price at which the same product is sold to another customer, such differential pricing can easily benefit both parties. Yet here price floors can play a particularly critical role in ensuring that the effects are indeed desirable for all those affected.

With differential pricing it is necessary to modify the price-floor rules somewhat. As before, price must exceed the pertinent marginal cost, for the same reasons as were given earlier. Moreover, the total-incremental revenue from the entire service must still cover the total-incremental cost of that service. But the charge for the lowest-priced units sold must now just exceed the average-incremental cost of all the units of the product that are sold *at that price*. It should be clear that if differential pricing satisfies this variant of our rules, it cannot exclude a more efficient rival, so that the purpose of the rule is achieved.

In practice, in telecommunications as in rail transportation, increased flexibility in regulation has led to more intensive bargaining between suppliers and their largest customers. This bargaining process has yielded contracts with attractive terms for the buyers. Most of these big customers are business firms, many of which compete directly with one another. If one succeeds in eliciting low telecommunications prices from its suppliers, other large customers are forced to demand similar treatment. The result is not only that buyers naturally desire special pricing terms; rather, they are *forced* to demand such prices. If they do not get them, they will find themselves at a marked competitive disadvantage.

It is easy to show that such differential prices, suitably selected, can benefit even the party that pays the higher relative price. As in our earlier numerical example, let the incremental costs of the first, second, and third units of output be $100, $80, and $30, respectively. That is, suppose that it costs the firm $100 to supply the first 1,000 message minutes per month along a given route, an additional $80 to

---

8. *See* MICHAEL K. KELLOGG, JOHN THORNE & PETER W. HUBER, FEDERAL TELECOMMUNICATIONS LAW 629–36 (Little, Brown & Co. 1992).

supply the next 1,000 message minutes, and so forth. Then the firm clearly requires a revenue of $180 to cover the cost of supplying 2,000 message minutes. So if only that amount is demanded, and there is no differential pricing in the sale of those units, the price must be $90 per 1,000 message minutes.

Now suppose that a large customer, A, offers to purchase an additional 1,000 message minutes along the route, but makes it clear that, because of competition, it can pay no more than $50 for this service. Since the incremental cost of the third 1,000 message minutes is only $30, this is clearly a profitable offer, yielding a net contribution of $20. Assuming that the supplier of telecommunications services earns no more profit than its cost of capital—which, as always in our discussion, is already included in the cost figures—the supply of 1,000 message minutes to customer A at its $50 offered price must reduce the prices paid by other customers. For the total cost that must now be covered by the firm is $100 plus $80 plus $30, or $210, of which $50 is covered by revenues from customer A. This leaves only $160 to be covered by the buyers of the first 2,000 units, so that the price they now have to pay is cut from $90 to $80 per 1,000 units as a result of customer A's bargain purchase under contract. Other customers can save $10 per 1,000 units because customer A's bargain purchase contributed $20 beyond the incremental cost of serving A, notwithstanding its comparatively low price.

Yet there is one danger here. Although the other customers must provide a revenue of only $160 if the agreement with customer A is concluded, those other customers must provide a revenue of $180 if the negotiations with customer A fail and the $20 contribution from that customer is lost as a result. The peril here is that while promising negotiations are under way with customer A, the optimistic telecommunications supplier will cut prices to other customers to $80. Yet if the anticipated contract with customer A never materializes, the $80 price to the other customers will not be compensatory. A pricing arrangement that prevents such violations of the price floor satisfies the rules of what has been called *anonymous equity*, a concept invented by Professor Robert D. Willig.[9] A pricing arrangement satisfies

9. Robert D. Willig, *Consumer Equity and Local Measured Service, in* PERSPEC-

anonymous equity if no sales of any product entail the receipt of a cross-subsidy from the buyers of other products of the same supplying firm and, in addition, if no sales entail a cross-subsidy from the sale of other units of the same product.

None of the observations in this section concerning differential pricing and services offered under contract is more than an application of the price-floor rules that this chapter has described. This section should thus be taken to illustrate the forms that may be assumed by the price-floor principles in practice and the complications that their application can encounter.

Conclusion

In this chapter, we have defined the key concepts of cross-subsidy and predatory pricing. We have shown the relevance of marginal cost and of the average-incremental cost of the entire product for the legitimate price floor in the competitive-market model, a floor that prevents both cross-subsidy and predatory pricing. In addition, we have shown that the price-floor rules require revenue to be sufficient to cover not only the average-incremental cost of each of the firm's products, but also the incremental cost of each possible combination of products supplied by the firm. Finally, we have explained the concept of anonymous equity and have shown how differential pricing can benefit all the firm's customers, even those not receiving the comparatively lower price.

TIVES ON LOCAL MEASURED SERVICE 71 (J.A. Baude *et al.* eds., Telecommunications Industry Workshop, Kansas City 1979). The concept was explored and analyzed thoroughly in Gerald R. Faulhaber & Stephen B. Levinson, *Subsidy-Free Prices and Anonymous Equity*, 71 AM. ECON. REV. 1083 (1981). For synopses of this literature, see ROGER SHERMAN, THE REGULATION OF MONOPOLY 158-62 (Cambridge Univ. Press 1989); BAUMOL, *supra* note 1, at 124–26.

6

Price Ceilings for Final Products

To DETERMINE THE PRICE CEILINGS prescribed by the competitive-market model for regulation, one first investigates the highest price that the firm can adopt in an effectively competitive arena—that is, a perfectly contestable market. This inquiry immediately gives us the required answer. In a perfectly contestable market, competitive behavior is imposed upon the incumbent firm by the threat of entry. Thus, the highest price or price combination that the incumbent can select is one that is just insufficient to attract the entry of new firms. Any price that would attract entrants is too high, for it could not persist in a perfectly contestable market. Therefore, such a price should be rejected by a regulator in the noncontestable regulated market, where the regulator's task is to impose the attributes of competitive behavior wherever the powers of competition are inadequate to prevent that result from being achieved automatically.

Stand-Alone Cost and the Combinatorial Cost Tests

This is where stand-alone cost (SAC) enters the matter. The stand-alone cost of product X is the cost that would be incurred by an efficient entrant if it were to produce X alone. That cost includes the required return to capital. Thus, by definition, any price of X that exceeds SAC_X would bring entrants flocking into the arena if that market were perfectly contestable, because such a price would yield more than the cost of the capital required to produce X. But any price that is an iota lower than SAC_X will be unprofitable for entrants, and it can therefore persist in a perfectly contestable market. It follows that stand-alone cost is the appropriate ceiling for price in a market regulated in accord with the competitive-market model.

That is not the end of the story, however. Like price floors, the price-ceiling standard applies not only to the products of the firm considered one at a time, but to every combination of the services of the firm.

In the case of price ceilings, the reason is more straightforward than it is for price floors. A potential producer of X is not constrained to produce only X. The prospective entrant can choose among product combinations, selecting the one most likely to be profitable. Suppose it decides to produce products W, X, and Z and to refrain from producing the incumbent's two other products, V and Y. Then the entry venture can be profitable only if the incumbent has priced W, X, and Z so that their combined revenues exceed the stand-alone cost of producing W, X, and Z, but with zero outputs of V and Y. Obviously, such prices of W, X, and Z could not survive the threat of entry in a perfectly contestable market. Hence, because those prices fail that combined stand-alone cost test, they too must be rejected by a regulator who follows the competitive-market model.

The combinatorial cost test, then, takes account of the likelihood that a prospective entrant will also be a multiproduct firm and that, like the incumbent, it will be able to benefit from any economies of scope that the technology of the arena makes possible. If the entrant can benefit from economies of scope, the stand-alone cost ceiling for the pertinent output combinations will ensure that the incumbent does not use such economies to achieve earnings that would not be permitted to it by the forces of an effectively competitive market.

To summarize, the combinatorial stand-alone price ceiling means that the prices of every combination of the firm's products must yield combined revenues not exceeding the corresponding stand-alone cost of the combination of products in question. Applied to the full set of products supplied by the firm, this rule dictates that the firm's total revenue must not exceed its total costs. This is the other half of the requirement that the firm be permitted to obtain earnings that equal but do not exceed the competitive earnings level. Although this sounds like an old-fashioned profit ceiling of the sort imposed under rate-base rate-of-return regulation, we will show presently that it is not. It can and should incorporate an automatic flexibility feature if the example of the competitive-market model is to be followed. But first, something must be said about the real-world practicality of administering the rules just described.

The Feasibility of Calculating Price Floors and Ceilings Versus the Feasibility of Calculating Ramsey Prices

It has been argued that the difficulty of calculation that has led to rejection of Ramsey pricing as a practical regulatory procedure also undermines the case for using an incremental-cost floor and a stand-alone cost ceiling. There are critical differences between the two approaches, however.

Ramsey price calculations cannot be carried out correctly without up-to-date knowledge of the demand elasticities and cross-elasticities for *every* product and pair of products of the firm. As is well known, provision of such a set of numbers, with constant updating, is generally an unachievable task. The floor-ceiling calculations described here and in Chapter 5 require no data related to demand. Only cost information is needed, and none of that information entails any cost allocation.

Moreover, the procedure advocated here does not require calculation in advance of *every* pertinent incremental and stand-alone cost. Only those few cost figures at issue in a particular hearing need be determined, and those are legitimately determined *ex post*. One can examine *in retrospect* whether a particular price fell short of the corresponding incremental cost or exceeded the corresponding stand-alone cost. That is why it has proved feasible in practice to carry out the requisite calculations, at least to a reasonable level of approximation.

Admittedly, in theory the ideal Ramsey prices are better for the public welfare than the broader range of options made available by the floor and the ceiling. But that superiority is surely unlikely for a surrogate for the Ramsey price that is based on elasticity and cross-elasticity figures that are likely in many instances to be poor approximations of the facts. And by removing all managerial discretion on prices, a regulatory Ramsey-pricing regime will surely undermine the responsiveness of pricing to changing market conditions.

Shortcuts and Approximations

As we noted earlier, full execution of the combinatorial requirement of the stand-alone cost ceiling can be a mind-boggling task that threatens to make the entire procedure impractical. This is not the place to describe the shortcuts and approximations that have been devised to make it easier and cheaper to calculate stand-alone costs. But experience in railroad regulation has shown that such calculations are feasible, and the determination of such cost figures has become a fairly routine activity, with firms specializing in the requisite calculations.

In practice, there are straightforward ways to reduce the complications of the combinatorial test problem in litigation and regulatory proceedings. First, the firm's services can be aggregated into a smaller number of sets, each set composed perhaps of a group of products sharing common facilities. If the company's products are grouped into five to ten broad product lines, the task of calculating stand-alone costs for each combination of these products is not overwhelming.

This shortcut is helpful even though it is sometimes necessary to carry the disaggregation somewhat further. A customer complaining about high prices, for example, may admit that the revenues of none of the aggregate groups or group combinations exceed the corresponding stand-alone cost ceiling, but can charge that the ceiling rule nonetheless is violated for a smaller subgroup. In such a case, rather than requiring the regulated firm to perform the daunting task of calculating stand-alone cost ceilings for every product combination's revenues any time a change in prices is proposed, the complaining parties can (and should) be asked to identify the particular product combinations for which they believe the ceiling is violated. This exercise is equivalent to the potential entrants selecting the combination of products that appears to promise the greatest profits. The complaining party must be discouraged from arbitrarily proliferating the list of suspect product combinations. Regulators can accomplish this by requiring the complainant to proffer some preliminary evidence supporting its accusation.

The regulated firm can then be required in turn to provide the regulator with stand-alone cost figures for the combinations of products whose prices require further examination.

Concern over estimation of stand-alone cost figures can be ascribed to unfamiliarity with the concept. Despite the Interstate Commerce Commission (ICC) rate cases in which railroads and shippers have used stand-alone costs for nearly a decade, relatively little has been done along those lines before other regulatory agencies, particularly in telecommunications.[1] This state of affairs may be changing; thus, consulting economists have demonstrated the feasibility of econometric estimation of stand-alone costs for third-class mail in postal-rate proceedings,[2] and the staff of the Federal Energy Regulatory Commission has begun considering the desirability of using stand-alone cost to regulate prices charged by oil pipelines.[3]

It is also helpful that stand-alone costs can be calculated indirectly with the aid of the much more familiar concept of long-run incremental cost. Such cost numbers have been submitted to the FCC for several decades.[4] They were also exhaustively examined in antitrust litigation

1. The seminal ICC decisions announcing the stand-alone cost test are *Ex Parte* No. 347 (Sub.-No.1), Coal Rate Guidelines—Nationwide (unpublished decision issued Feb. 8, 1983); Coal Rate Guidelines, Nationwide, 1 I.C.C.2d 520 (1985). ICC decisions implementing the stand-alone cost test include Potomac Elec. Power Co. *v.* Consolidated Rail Corp., 367 I.C.C. 532 (1983), *aff'd*, Potomac Elec. Power Co. *v.* ICC, 744 F.2d 185 (D.C. Cir. 1984); Omaha Pub. Power Dist. *v.* Burlington N. R.R., 3 I.C.C.2d 123 (1986), *aff'd*, 3 I.C.C.2d 853 (1987); Arkansas Power & Light Co. *v.* Burlington N. R.R., 3 I.C.C.2d 757 (1987); Metropolitan Edison Co. *v.* Conrail, 5 I.C.C.2d 385 (1989); Bituminous Coal—Hiawatha, Utah, to Moapa, Nevada ("Nevada Power"), 6 I.C.C.2d 1 (1989); Coal Trading Corp. *v.* Baltimore & Ohio R.R., 6 I.C.C.2d 361 (1990). For a lucid summary of the ICC's experience using stand-alone cost, see Burlington N. R.R. *v.* ICC, 985 F.2d 589, 595–99 (D.C. Cir. 1993) (Williams, J.).

2. *See* Thomas M. Lenard, Monica M. Bettendorf & Stephen McGonegal, *Stand-Alone Costs, Ramsey Prices, and Postal Rates*, 4 J. REG. ECON. 243 (1992).

3. *See* Comments of the Association of Oil Pipe Lines on Commission Staff Proposal, Revisions to Oil Pipeline Regulations Pursuant to the Energy Policy Act of 1992, Dkt. No. RM93-11-000 (filed before FERC May 3, 1993) (containing affidavit by Prof. Robert D. Willig discussing application of stand-alone cost test to oil pipelines).

4. *See* American Tel. & Tel. Co., Manual and Procedures for the Allocation of Costs, Notice of Proposed Rulemaking, CC Dkt. No. 79-245, 78 F.C.C.2d 1296, 1301–03 ¶¶ 17–20 (1980) (describing AT&T's "Seven-Way Cost Study"); American Tel. & Tel. Co., Investigation into the Lawfulness of Tariff F.C.C. No. 267, Offering a Dataphone Digital Serv. Between Five Cities, Dkt. No. 20288, 62 F.C.C.2d 774, 782–83 ¶¶ 21–26 (1977); American Tel. & Tel. Co., Long Lines Dept., Revision of Tariff FCC No. 260

in the telecommunications industry in the 1980s.[5] More recently, both AT&T and Pacific Bell have submitted incremental cost numbers to the California Public Utilities Commission in the *Readyline* case.[6] Long-run incremental cost calculations have also been endorsed in principle or used in practice in a number of state regulatory proceedings.[7]

Although disputes continue about the details of the calculation procedures, incremental cost is now widely accepted as an operational concept, and its calculation methods are well understood. This familiarity is fortunate for the stand-alone cost calculation, because stand-alone cost can be deduced directly from the incremental cost for an appropriately selected set of services. The set of services for which the incremental cost must be calculated is determined without difficulty from the combination of services for which the stand-alone cost number is desired.

For this purpose we must first define *complementary subsets*, S_1 and S_2, of the set S of goods or services constituting the firm's product line. Suppose a company produces a set S composed of six services, A, B, C, D, E, and F. If the pertinent subset S_1 is constituted by services A and C, then the complementary subset S_2 is defined as the subset of all the remaining services, in this case the four services B, D, E, and F. That is, two subsets, S_1 and S_2, of any set S (the full set of services of the firm) are defined to be complementary if $S_1 + S_2 = S$.

We now prove that the stand-alone cost of any subset S_1 is equal to the firm's total cost minus the incremental cost of the complementary

Private Line Serv., Series 5000 (TELPAK), Mem. Op. & Order, Dkt. No. 18128, 61 F.C.C.2d 587, 627–33 ¶¶ 124–37 (1976); American Tel. & Tel. Co. & Assoc. Bell Sys. Cos., Charges for Interstate & Foreign Comm. Serv., Dkt. No. 16258, 18 F.C.C.2d 761, 763–64 ¶¶ 7–9 (1969). *See also* STEPHEN G. BREYER, REGULATION AND ITS REFORM 305–08 (Harvard Univ. Press 1982) (discussing FCC's analysis of long-run incremental cost in Docket 18128).

5. Southern Pac. Comm. Co. *v.* American Tel. & Tel. Co., 556 F. Supp. 825, 922–27 (D.D.C. 1983), *aff'd*, 740 F.2d 980 (D.C. Cir.), *cert. denied*, 470 U.S. 1005 (1984); MCI *v.* American Tel. & Tel. Co., 708 F.2d 1081, 1115, 1119–23 (7th Cir.), *cert. denied*, 464 U.S. 891 (1983).

6. AT&T Communications of Ca., Inc., 38 C.P.U.C.2d 126, 134–37 (1990).

7. *See, e.g.*, People *ex rel.* O'Malley v. Illinois Commerce Comm'n, 239 Ill. App. 3d 368, 606 N.E.2d 1282 (1993); Promulgation of Rules for Establishment of Alternative Regulation for Large Local Exchange Telephone Companies, 1993 Ohio PUC LEXIS 35, at *27–29, 140 P.U.R.4th 23 (1993); American Can Co. *v.* Lobdell, 55 Or. App. 451, 638 P.2d 1152 (1982). *See also* OR. REV. STAT. § 759.250(4)(b) (1991).

subset S_2. Let $T(...)$ represent the total cost of some set or subset of the firm's services, using a to represent the size of the output of service A, and so forth. Then we have the following definitions:

Total cost (TC) of the firm $= T(S) = T(a,b,c,d,e,f)$;

Incremental cost (IC) of subset $S_1 = T(a,b,c,d,e,f) - T(0,b,0,d,e,f)$

$\qquad = T(S) - T(S - S_1) = T(S) - T(S_2)$;

Stand-alone cost (SAC) of subset S_2 (complementary to S_1)

$\qquad = T(0,b,0,d,e,f) = T(S_2)$.

Examining these three definitions of TC, IC, and SAC, respectively, we see at once that

$$IC(S_1) = TC(S) - SAC(S_2), \text{ or} \qquad (6.1)$$

$$SAC(S_2) = TC(S) - IC(S_1). \qquad (6.2)$$

In words, this equation asserts that to find the stand-alone cost for any preselected subset, S_2, of the services of a firm, we need only determine the complementary subset S_1, calculate its incremental cost, and subtract that incremental cost from the firm's total cost. That total cost is the known total of the expenses incurred by the firm in the period during which the output quantities a, b, c, d, e, and f are produced, including the flow equivalent of its capital outlays. Thus, one obtains the SAC figures as an absolutely free bonus when one calculates the incremental costs of the complementary subsets of the firm's services.

Admittedly, a complication arises if the firm is not an efficient supplier, for then the TC, IC, and SAC figures are all likely to be excessive. If the firm is inefficient, it becomes necessary to adjust its cost figures downward by appropriate amounts. It would be disingenuous to pretend that this is an easy task. But this problem is not unique to use of stand-alone cost and incremental cost. On the contrary, exactly the same task must be performed whatever the cost figures that are used to regulate prices, even if fully distributed costs are used for the purpose, unless regulators wish to invite the regulated firm to be as wasteful as it cares to be and to do so with impunity.

One Test or Two for Floors and Ceilings?

Another relationship that can facilitate the administration of the program of price floors and ceilings is a simple theorem that corresponds to Equation (6.2). It asserts that if the regulated firm passes the combinatorial price-floor tests and earns no more than competitive profits, then the price-ceiling tests must automatically be passed. The result also works the other way: if the firm's prices pass the combinatorial price-ceiling tests and it earns exactly competitive profits overall, then the price-floor test is redundant. In other words, the firm's prices need only be subjected to one set of tests.

The intuitive explanation is straightforward. If a company earns no more and no less than competitive profits, any shortfall in the revenues from one of its products, X, must be exactly offset by excess revenues from another product, or set of products, Y. With no such offset, excess revenues from any one product must mean excess total profits, and insufficient revenues from that one product must mean company losses. Thus, if profits are just at the competitive level and there is no product that yields excess revenues, then we know that no product can conceivably yield inadequate revenues. The same reasoning applies in the other direction—the absence of any product with inadequate revenues precludes the existence of any product with excessive revenues.

Formal proof of the proposition is also straightforward. Let the firm produce two products, X and Y, and let $TC(x,y)$ be the total cost of producing them when quantities x,y are supplied. Let p_X be the price of X, and so forth. Then, the competitive overall-profit requirement is

$$p_X x + p_Y y = TC(x,y). \tag{6.3}$$

The total service incremental-cost floor for the price of X requires

$$p_X x \geq TC(x,y) - TC(0,y),\tag{6.4}$$

which, when subtracted from Equation (6.3), immediately tells us that the price of Y cannot violate the stand-alone cost ceiling:

$$p_Y y \leq TC(0,y).\tag{6.5}$$

Similarly, subtraction of Equation (6.5) from Equation (6.3) immediately yields Equation (6.4), so that if the price of Y does not violate the ceiling, the price of X cannot violate the floor, which is what was to be shown.

Rate-of-Return Regulation and Cross-Subsidy

Although not directly germane to the issue of price ceilings, it is appropriate to mention a problem engendered by the regulation of telecommunications prices through a ceiling on profits—that is, through the traditional rate-base rate-of-return approach. As suggested earlier, cross-subsidy is prospectively a serious impediment to the emergence and survival of competition. A regulated firm wishing to keep out or destroy competitors can, if permitted, set uncompensatory prices for services in which it faces rivals, making up for the shortfall from its high profits on those of its services in which it enjoys a monopoly. In the absence of a limit on profits, however, such a step is costly because the cross-subsidies necessarily entail a sacrifice of monopoly profits.

Observers have often argued that the incentive for such cross-subsidies is enhanced by profit-ceiling regulation, for the profit ceiling provides the firm with a pool of unused potential profits that, in the absence of cross-subsidy, regulation does not permit it to exploit fully. If so, the firm can perhaps accept losses on its competitive services with greater equanimity, pricing those services at levels that make sense only as means to harm competitors. For the regulated firm can make up for those losses out of its untapped profits, if clever accounting and legal arguments can persuade the regulator to permit this on the grounds that earnings will otherwise be inadequate.

This argument, although not universally accepted, certainly constitutes an additional reason for discomfort with the regime of rate-of-
return regulation or any close substitute.

Price Ceilings and Productivity Growth

Price ceilings for final products have a larger defect: they undermine
any inducement for productivity or efficiency improvements. As
constructed, they appear to require the sort of preset total revenue
figure that rate-base rate-of-return regulation sought virtually to
guarantee. That old regulatory regime strove for a cost-plus
arrangement analogous to the compensation formulas common in
purchase contracts by government agencies, under which the seller is
permitted to charge a price equal to product cost—usually, fully
distributed cost (however calculated) plus a "fair" markup. Being
promised no more and no less than this amount, the vendor was
deprived of any incentive for cost saving, growth in efficiency, or cost-
reducing innovation. The older regulatory arrangement for pricing the
final products of natural monopolists probably produced similar
consequences.

This problem of providing incentives for productivity improvement
is slightly alleviated, though not eliminated, by switching from fully
distributed cost to stand-alone cost as the basis for the price ceiling.
For, interpreted rigidly, a regime of price ceilings predicated on combinatorial stand-alone costs permits the regulated enterprise to earn no
more in total than the stand-alone cost of its entire product line. That
is, the firm is never permitted to recoup more than total cost, including
the cost of its capital.

Yet, for two reasons, elements of this arrangement entail greater
flexibility than that permitted by rate-base rate-of-return regulation of
prices. First, prices are no longer fixed by the regulator, who now
merely enjoins the firm to price no higher than the stand-alone cost
ceiling. Prices below that figure are deemed perfectly acceptable,
provided they do not violate the cost floor.

Second, and more important, the pertinent stand-alone cost is not the actual cost incurred by the regulated firm, but rather the cost that would be incurred *by the entry of a hypothetical efficient entrant*. This means that the regulated firm is not condemned to an automatic reduction in its price ceiling if it succeeds in reducing *its own* costs, because such improvement in efficiency does not reduce the costs of the hypothetical entrant on which the ceiling is based.

Use of a cost-reducing innovation by the regulated firm does not normally disclose the details of its technology to the marketplace, or at least does not disclose them immediately. It is also well established in antitrust law that the innovating monopolist has no legal obligation to share its proprietary information with its rivals.[8] Of course, if there is instantaneous diffusion to rivals of the proprietary knowledge embodied in the cost-reducing innovation, then a hypothetical entrant can be expected to have its own stand-alone cost lowered by the incumbent's innovation. But when there is a lag in the diffusion of proprietary information to competitors, then a cost advantage will accrue to the incumbent for at least some period of time. Thus, under the regime of price ceilings based on stand-alone cost, the firm retains pricing freedom and some incentive for economy that was absent under the earlier regulatory approach.

Still, it is a disincentive to investment in research and development for a firm that achieves a revolutionary innovation to be denied a corresponding increase in its net revenues, as the stand-alone cost ceiling for the firm's entire product line appears to do. Moreover, such a rigid profit constraint violates the precepts of the competitive-market model for regulation, because the competitive market *does* permit the successful innovator to earn especially generous profits. Next, we will examine how this problem can be and has been dealt with.

---

8. *See, e.g.*, Foremost Pro Color, Inc. *v.* Eastman Kodak Co., 703 F.2d 534, 545 (9th Cir. 1983), *cert. denied*, 465 U.S. 1038 (1984); Berkey Photo, Inc. *v.* Eastman Kodak Co., 603 F.2d 263, 279–85 (2d Cir. 1979), *cert. denied*, 444 U.S. 1093 (1980). *See also* J. Gregory Sidak, *Debunking Predatory Innovation*, 83 COLUM. L. REV. 1121, 1146–48 (1983).

The Operation of Price Caps

To provide the required incentive for efficiency, innovation, and productivity growth that is absent under a rigidly fixed profit ceiling, a flexible version of the price ceiling has been devised and widely adopted.[9] This arrangement, called "price caps," builds on a virtue that derives from the phenomenon of regulatory lag—that is, the general delay in the responses of regulators to changes in cost or market conditions.[10] The pertinent delay here is the regulator's time lag in adjusting permitted prices to changes in costs.

Suppose that the firm's prices are set on the basis of current costs, and the firm succeeds in reducing those costs substantially. Suppose further that, say, two years elapse before regulators require the firm to cut its prices correspondingly. Then the firm will enjoy two years of superior profits as its reward for improved efficiency. That process mimics a competitive market, where a cost-cutting innovator enjoys superior but temporary profits. Those higher profits end when rivals introduce their own cost-reducing innovations, wiping out the competitive advantage temporarily enjoyed by the earlier innovator.

The competitive-market model suggests that the built-in regulatory lag at the heart of the price-cap approach must be substantial, because otherwise firms will have no effective incentive to undertake the heavy costs and risks of innovation, and society will be the loser. On the other hand, the lag, like the life of a patent, must not be infinite, lest the consuming public be forced to forgo the benefits of lower prices that the competitive market normally transmits to it.

Regulatory lag thus supplies the incentive required to elicit innovation and productivity growth, with one critical exception. When inflation is substantial, regulatory lag delays the adjustment of output

9. Perhaps the first systematic proposal for such a regime was offered in 1968 in William J. Baumol, *Reasonable Rules for Rate Regulation, Plausible Policies for an Imperfect World, in* ALMARIN PHILIPS & OLIVER E. WILLIAMSON, PRICES: ISSUES IN THEORY, PRACTICE AND PUBLIC POLICY (Univ. of Pennsylvania Press 1968). *See also* William J. Baumol, *Productivity Incentive Clauses and Rate Adjustment for Inflation*, PUB. UTIL. FORTNIGHTLY, vol. 110, no. 2, at 11 (July 22, 1982).

10. *See* Policy and Rules Concerning Rates for Dominant Carriers, Rep. & Order & Second Further Notice of Proposed Rulemaking, CC Dkt. No. 87-313, 4 F.C.C. Rec. 2873 (1989) [hereinafter *AT&T Price Caps Order*].

prices to compensate for inflationary increases in nominal input costs. This delay squeezes the profits of the regulated firm and undercuts both its incentive and its ability to invest in innovation. To deal with the inflation problem, the price-cap arrangement uses the following procedures:

1. An initial price ceiling is determined on the basis of standalone cost or a defensible proxy.

2. The price ceiling is permitted to rise automatically each year by a percentage equal to the rise of some widely accepted index of inflation, such as the consumer price index (CPI), after subtracting some number, X, from the percentage increase in that price index. The arrangement is often referred to as "CPI $-$ X."

3. X is calculated from the industry's rate of productivity growth in the past, or as a target rate of productivity growth for the industry.

The logic of price caps is straightforward. Productivity growth offsets inflation in the costs incurred by any firm. If wages and input prices rise by 7 percent, for example, but productivity rises by 5 percent (so that the input quantities required to produce a given output fall 5 percent from those amounts in the previous year), then the per-unit cost of the firm will rise only by the difference between the input-price rise and the productivity offset—that is, 7 minus 5 percent, or 2 percent.

The consequence is now straightforward. Continuing with the example, suppose that on the basis of past growth performance in the industry, X had been chosen to equal 3 percent. Then, under price caps, the price ceiling would be permitted to rise by CPI $-$ X, or by $7 - 3 = 4$ percent. Our regulated firm, having exceeded the 3 percent productivity growth target by achieving a 5 percent increase in productivity, then experiences a 2 percent nominal cost rise, but is permitted a 4 percent rise in price. That is, the firm is permitted a percentage increase in the profit margin on its product that precisely equals the amount by which its productivity performance exceeded the target.

The opposite is experienced by a firm whose productivity performance falls short of the target. Suppose that another regulated firm manages barely to increase productivity by 2 percent. Its costs then rise by $7 - 2 = 5$ percent; but its price cap, like that of the more successful innovator, only rises by CPI $- X = 4$ percent. In sum, under price caps, the firm whose productivity increase exceeds the norm will enjoy higher returns exactly commensurate with its achievement, while the firm with poor productivity performance will automatically be penalized, correspondingly.

That is all that has to be said about the price-cap approach to regulatory price ceilings, noting again that it provides incentives much like those of the competitive market. This is yet another feature of the regulatory price rules described in this monograph that, like the other provisions, follows the competitive-market model.[11]

In practice, however, one other proviso has normally been included. Rather than setting price caps item by item, regulators have aggregated the products of the regulated firm into baskets of services, such as household services or 800 services, that warrant similar regulatory treatment. Then, only the *average* of the prices of the items in each basket is required to satisfy the price-cap ceiling.[12] The purpose of this provision is to increase still further the domain of price-setting freedom of the regulated firm and to prevent the rules from having unexpectedly severe consequences for any one narrowly defined service—an occurrence that can otherwise be expected to happen somewhere, simply by happenstance.

11. For further analysis of price caps, see BRIDGER M. MITCHELL & INGO VOGELSANG, TELECOMMUNICATIONS PRICING: THEORY AND PRACTICE 167–75, 276–85 (Cambridge Univ. Press 1991); Ronald R. Braeutigam & John C. Panzar, *Effects of the Change from Rate of Return to Price Cap Regulation*, 83 AM. ECON. REV. PAPERS & PROC. 191 (1993).

12. *See AT&T Price Caps Order, supra* note 10, at 3051–65 ¶¶ 359–86; MITCHELL & VOGELSANG, *supra* note 11, at 168–69.

Constrained-Market Pricing Versus Rate-Base Rate-of-Return Regulation

The Interstate Commerce Commission has dubbed the regulatory approach outlined in this chapter "constrained-market pricing," or CMP.[13] In our discussion of the combinatorial character of the price-ceiling tests earlier in this chapter, we observed that the stand-alone cost ceiling for the totality of services of the regulated firm amounts to the requirement that the firm earn no more than its cost of capital. Thus, it would appear that constrained-market pricing drives rate-base rate-of-return regulation (ROR) out the front door and then lets it in again by the back entrance. In both theory and practice, however, the two approaches to regulation are very different.

First, ROR has traditionally been used to minimize the freedom of choice of management in setting prices, with firms typically being required to propose new prices and justify them in advance with evidence that they do not violate the ROR requirement. Under constrained-market pricing, management is given considerable freedom in price setting; in some arenas, any price proposal by the firm is presumed to be legitimate and may be instituted with minimum delay, objections to those prices being entertained only *ex post*.

Second, CMP regulation is freed from the legalistic and near-theological battles over the proper methods for full distribution of costs. Such battles made ROR regulation most damaging to the public interest.

Third, so far as we are aware, litigation under CMP has never focused on the rate of return of the regulated enterprise. Rather, complaining parties have argued that the price of some service has, or the prices of some limited combination of services have, violated the specified floors or ceilings.

Fourth, the price-cap element of CMP regulation has permitted and encouraged firms to earn more than their cost of capital by means of the flexibility built into the ceilings. Such flexibility effectively

---

13. Burlington N. R.R. *v.* ICC, 985 F.2d 589 (D.C. Cir. 1993) (Williams, J.). *See also* WILLIAM J. BAUMOL, JOHN C. PANZAR & ROBERT D. WILLIG, CONTESTABLE MARKETS AND THE THEORY OF INDUSTRY STRUCTURE 504–07 (Harcourt Brace Jovanovich rev. ed. 1988) (discussing ICC decisions).

undercuts any attempt to transform CMP into ROR; most important, it restores the incentive for innovation and growth in efficiency that ROR so effectively hampered.

In short there simply has been no resemblance in actual regulatory hearings and proceedings between the scenarios played out under CMP and those common under ROR.

Conclusion

In this chapter we have explained the relevance of stand-alone cost, and of the combinatorial cost test, to the optimal price ceilings for the final products of a regulated monopolist. These price ceilings are more readily calculated in practice than are Ramsey prices. Indeed, at least some regulators are familiar with price ceilings based on stand-alone cost, and many other regulators or courts are familiar with long-run incremental cost. The familiarity of regulators with the latter is significant because the stand-alone cost of any subset of the products supplied by the regulated firm is calculated automatically if one knows the firm's total costs and the incremental cost of the complementary subset of the firm's other products. We have also examined how price ceilings can impede productivity growth, and how the price-cap approach ameliorates this problem.

7

The Pricing of Inputs Sold to Competitors

ONE OF THE MOST VEXING ISSUES facing the regulator of local telephone service is the pricing of access to the local loop when that service is supplied by the local exchange carrier to interexchange carriers with which the LEC competes in intraLATA toll services. Access has two significant and pertinent attributes. First, access is an intermediate good—an input used in the supply of a final product, intra-LATA toll service. Second, this input is produced by the LEC and used not only by itself, but also by its rivals in the market for the final product. This issue arises generically whenever a firm, X, is the only supplier of an input used both by itself and by a rival to provide some final product. If X charges its rival more for the input than it implicitly charges itself, it will have handicapped that rival's ability to compete with X, perhaps seriously. The reverse will be true if regulation forces X to charge the rival less for the input than X charges itself.

This intermediate-goods problem can distort the efficient division of responsibilities between the LEC and the IXCs in supplying competitive telecommunications services. An excessive price for access handicaps the IXCs in their effort to attract a share of the competitive final-product business in question. Correspondingly, too low an access price handicaps the LEC. Either such price distortion can direct some of the business in question to an inefficient supplier. This kind of inefficiency can also be expressed in terms of the profits the LEC earns when it supplies access to itself and when it supplies access to the

IXCs. If the LEC charges the IXCs so high a price that any sale yields a large incremental profit, but the LEC forgoes some of this profit when it uses access in its own sale of intraLATA toll services, then the LEC will have set an indefensibly low price for its final product. It will thus constitute a competitive impediment for the IXCs. Thus the problem is to ensure an appropriate relationship between the profits the LEC earns from providing access to itself and those it earns from selling access to its competitors in the final-product market.

What is the proper relation between these two profit figures? The unambiguous answer that this chapter proposes may appear unfamiliar and to have been invented especially to address the pricing of intermediate inputs such as access. On the contrary, the optimal input-pricing rule that we will describe is merely another use of the incremental-cost principles that achieve economic efficiency. The role of opportunity cost is given special emphasis because of its relevance to the current issue.

A critical requirement for economic efficiency is that the price of any product be no lower than that product's marginal cost or its average-incremental cost. Economic analysis emphasizes that the pertinent marginal cost as well as the average-incremental cost must include all *opportunity costs* incurred by the supplier in providing the product. Here opportunity cost refers to all potential earnings that the supplying firm forgoes, either by providing inputs of its own rather than purchasing them, or by offering services to competitors that force it to relinquish business to those rivals, and thus to forgo the profits on that lost business. In a competitive market, price always includes compensation for such opportunity costs—for example, for the interest forgone by the firm when it supplies funds from retained earnings rather than borrowing them from a bank. The optimal input-pricing rule states simply that the price of an input should equal its average-incremental cost, *including all pertinent incremental opportunity costs*. That is:

optimal input price = the input's direct per unit incremental cost + the opportunity cost to the input supplier of the sale of a unit of input.

This chapter will explain the logic and consequences of that rule. In the following discussion, the term "direct costs" will refer to all costs that, from the point of view of the supplier firm, are not opportunity costs.

The Efficient Component-Pricing Rule

The literature on the economics of price regulation indicates that the pricing principle just described can guide the choice of efficient access charges. This pricing principle—variously known as the *efficient component-pricing rule*, the *imputation requirement*, the *principle of competitive equality*, or the *parity principle*—is merely a variant of the elementary principles for efficiency in pricing that have been discussed already. This rule applies to the sale of an input—a component K of the final product—by a supplier X of both the component and the final product. The purchasing firm Y uses the component to produce the same final product as X and sells that final product in competition with X. Here Y is itself assumed to make the remaining components (other than K) of the final product. If X sells component K to Y, then Y is enabled to compete with X in selling the final product. When X sells component K to Y, either voluntarily or pursuant to regulatory mandate, what price should X charge for component K?

To answer this question, we will use an example from rail transportation rather than telecommunications because, in our experience, the logic of the issue seems to be grasped more easily with the aid of the rail analogy. As we will show, however, regulators already have applied this logic to telecommunications markets. Consider then two railroads, X and Y, that operate along parallel routes from an intermediate point B to a destination point C, as illustrated in Figure 7.1. Railroad X owns the only tracks extending from the origin point A to the intermediate point B. In this case, the final product is transportation all the way from A to C. Competing railroad Y, also a proprietor of tracks from B to C, can be expected in these circumstances to apply to railroad X for "interconnection" from A to B, seeking to rent trackage rights along that route from its rival. If the transaction is completed, Y (like X) will be able to ship all the way

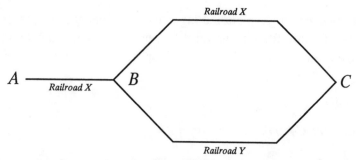

Figure 7.1 The Trackage Rights-Pricing Problem

from *A* to *C*; in regulatory parlance, *X* then is called the landlord railroad and *Y* is called the tenant. Regulators commonly have been requested by prospective tenants to force a landlord to grant them trackage rights. For obvious reasons, the regulatory agency usually has been asked to set the rental fee as well.

The sale of access by a LEC to an IXC that is a horizontal competitor of the LEC in the market for intraLATA toll services is precisely analogous to the grant of trackage rights by the landlord to the tenant railroad. Access is an input to the final product, interexchange telecommunication, and is not essentially different from the purchase of any other intermediate input. Setting a price for access to the local loop in telecommunications is, therefore, precisely analogous to setting of the rental fee for trackage rights. More generally, the pricing of access is analogous to pricing any product component in comparable circumstances.

The efficient component-pricing rule has already advanced from theory to practice in the United States and abroad. The Interstate Commerce Commission (ICC) has applied the rule in several railroad rate cases.[1] In October 1989, the California Public Utilities Commission embraced the rule in its reform of regulation of local exchange carriers.[2] Most recently, the High Court of New Zealand

1. For example, see the quartet of cases known as *Compensation I* through *IV*, St. Louis S.W. Ry.—Trackage Rights over Missouri Pac. R.R.—Kansas City to St. Louis, 1 I.C.C.2d 776 (1984), 4 I.C.C.2d 668 (1987), 5 I.C.C.2d 525 (1989), 8 I.C.C.2d 80 (1991).
2. Alternative Regulatory Framework for Local Exchange Carriers, Invest. No. 87-11-033, 33 C.P.U.C.2d 43, 107 P.U.R.4th 1 (1989).

adopted the rule in antitrust litigation between Clear Communication, Ltd. and the former government telephone monopoly, Telecom Corporation of New Zealand, Ltd.[3]

The Traditional Regulatory Approach to Rental Fee Determination

Until recently, regulators often have approached the rental-fee decision in the manner suggested by the following example. Let the direct average-incremental cost incurred by landlord X as a result of Y's use of its track be AIC dollars per train. This is the additional cost per train incurred by the landlord railroad—including track wear and tear, additional planning, and administrative cost—as a result of the tenant's use of the landlord's tracks.

Suppose that because of economies of scale, total revenues must exceed the sum of the incremental costs of the two types of traffic if X is to break even. Suppose further that, in the absence of trackage rights, the traffic from A to C had yielded X a net contribution toward the shortfall (that is, total incremental revenue minus incremental cost) of T, and assume that contribution T equals \$90 million per year. Finally, suppose that, after granting trackage rights, X is expected to retain two-thirds of the traffic from A to C, with the remaining traffic going to Y.

Assuming freight rates for shipments from A to C to be fixed, regulators generally have determined the proper rental fee for the trackage rights to consist of (1) a charge per train of railroad Y set equal to the (direct) average-incremental cost to X of handling Y's train, and (2) a supplement designed to leave X with exactly two-thirds of the \$90 million contribution that the traffic formerly provided. Under this regulatory rule, in other words, the landlord is granted its pro rata share of the contribution, in this case corresponding to its two-thirds expected share of the total traffic.

---

3. Clear Communications, Ltd. *v*. Telecom Corp. of New Zealand, Ltd., slip op. (H.C. Dec. 22, 1992). As of this writing the decision is on appeal to the New Zealand Court of Appeal. For an insightful discussion of the case, see James Farmer, *Transition from Protected Monopoly to Competition: The New Zealand Experiment*, 1 COMPETITION & CONSUMER L.J. 1 (1993).

This regulatory rule, however, violates economic efficiency. As we shall now show, it fails to compensate railroad X adequately for its common fixed costs; thus the rule distorts the efficient division of responsibilities between X and Y in supplying transport over the competitive segment BC.

The Efficient Component-Pricing Principle as a Requirement of Economic Efficiency: What Is the Efficiency Issue?

The efficient pricing principle for product components is required not only by the competitive-market standard for defensible behavior by an allegedly dominant firm. It is also a necessary condition for economic efficiency, and hence for promoting the public interest. That is, product-component prices that do not follow this principle constitute an incentive for inefficiency whose costs consumers will have to pay.

Another example shows the nature of the efficiency issue. Consider a pharmaceutical manufacturer X that is the sole supplier of a medical ingredient A on which it holds a patent. The final product may require other medical ingredients, capsule cases, packaging, and marketing services, all of which firm X also can provide, although it is not the only enterprise that can do so. Economic efficiency requires that capsule cases, packaging, retail marketing services, and so on each be supplied by those firms that can do the job most efficiently—that is, by means that minimize the costs of the labor, fuel, raw materials, and other inputs used in producing the components. The choice is often interpreted as a make-or-buy decision on the part of firm X, the supplier of patent-protected component A. Firm X should make the capsule cases, the packaging, and so on only if it is the most efficient supplier of these items. Otherwise, the public interest dictates that firm X buy those components from a rival supplier who can provide them more efficiently.

Whether firm X will make the efficient choice voluntarily depends on the relative price of the competing suppliers of the capsule cases (and the other product inputs). If their price when offered by a rival supplier is lower than the cost at which firm X can make capsule cases for itself, then X will be motivated to buy the cases rather than make them.

Efficiency in pricing requires the capsules to be priced so that X will find it profitable to select the more efficient provider to manufacture the capsules—supplying the capsules itself if and only if it is the more efficient supplier. In telecommunications services, the analogous problem is to price access so that the job of carrying intraLATA traffic goes to the more efficient of the competing carriers.

Efficiency of the Component-Pricing Rule and the Competitive-Market Model

In brief, the optimal component-pricing rule asserts that the rent that tenant railroad Y should pay per train is the entire average-incremental cost incurred by each train traversing landlord railroad X's route AB, *including any incremental opportunity cost* that the passage of Y's train imposes on X. Expressed in this way, the rule is entirely familiar to economists, and its logic will be virtually self-evident to them, except for its focus on average-incremental cost rather than marginal cost.

The efficiency of this optimal component-pricing rule is confirmed indirectly by the fact that it yields a price level set in precisely the same way it would be in a perfectly competitive or a perfectly contestable market. To see this, imagine a set of landlords competing to rent retail space to tenants. Suppose further, as is often true, that if no suitable tenant can be found, the space can be used for the landlord's own profitable retailing establishment. No landlord who can use the property in this way will rent it to anyone for less than the direct incremental cost of the tenant's occupation of the property *plus the opportunity cost to the landlord* of the rental arrangement. If the landlord can earn \$90,000 by using the property, the tenant will be required to make good the \$90,000 that is forgone by renting the property. The same argument applies whether the opportunity cost is incurred because landlord and tenant compete for space or because they compete for customers.

Consequently, even in the most competitive of markets, no landlord will rent for a fee less than that given by the efficient component-pricing rule. Moreover, if competition abounds—that is, if a profusion of alternative properties are available to the tenant on comparable terms—the tenant will pay no more than that. (In practice, of course, the tenant can be expected to spend a small amount more than that, in order to induce the landlord to rent rather than use the property.)

Since, in the absence of externalities, we expect competitive prices to be consistent with economic efficiency, the preceding argument establishes a presumption that the component-pricing rule is indeed optimal. This is also made clear by our railroad example, which will now be used to show how the optimal input price is calculated.

Recall from Figure 7.1 that in our illustration only railroad X offers transportation from A to B (route AB) and then to C (route BXC). Its competitor, railroad Y, also offers transportation from B to C (route BYC), and it wishes to serve shippers from A as well by renting trackage rights along X's route AB. By obtaining interconnection over route AB, railroad Y will be able to offer shippers seamless transportation service from A to C, which is our illustrative final product. Suppose the competitive price to shippers for transport from A to C is $10 per ton, and X's incremental cost along each of its two route segments, AB and BXC, is $3 per ton. Thus, on its carriage of shipments from A to C, landlord X earns a net contribution toward its common fixed costs equal to the final-product price minus its two incremental costs—that is,

$$X\text{'s earned contribution} = \$10 - \$3 - \$3 = \$4$$

for every ton of freight X carries over the full route from A to C.

In a competitive market, what will railroad X charge railroad Y for permitting the latter to haul a ton of freight over X's route AB? Assume for simpler exposition that each ton of freight carried from B to C by Y means that one less ton is transported by X. Then, even if there are other railroads in a position similar to X's, none will rent Y their tracks unless Y pays them enough to compensate for the cost of the lost profit that Y's interconnection will impose on them. This cost includes the direct incremental cost—wear and tear of X's tracks, fuel if X is required to supply the engine, and so on—a sum that we take to be $3 in our example. But full compensation for interconnection also requires that Y pay for the incremental *opportunity cost* its traffic imposes upon X—that is, the loss of $4 of net contribution toward common fixed costs that X incurs for every ton of business that Y diverts from X by using X's tracks. Thus, the competitive-market standard requires that the price of trackage rights (or, more generally, of interconnection) must also satisfy the efficient component-pricing rule. In our example, the direct per-unit incremental cost to railroad X of permitting use of its route AB is $3 per ton. Railroad X's per-unit opportunity cost is its loss of $4 per ton of net contribution toward its common fixed costs. Thus, the efficient component price for granting railroad Y interconnection over route AB is $7 per ton—the price that would emerge in a competitive market.

Direct Discussion of the Role of Component Pricing in Promoting Efficiency

We come now to the critical role that the component-pricing principle has in promoting economic efficiency. Continuing with our railroad example, we will show now that if the price of the component provided by landlord railroad X is set in accord with this pricing rule, then the two participating railroads will face incentives that automatically assign the business over route AB to the supplier who can provide it with the least use of fuel, labor, and other valuable inputs. But if the rental payment for the landlord's component—in this case, X's tracks over route AB—is set at a price below that required by the efficient component-pricing principle, the requirements of economic efficiency will be violated.

Economic efficiency requires that the competitive segment of the service be performed only by efficient suppliers—that is, by those suppliers whose incremental costs incurred to supply the service are the lowest available. For this goal to be realized, it must be possible for the more efficient suppliers to make a net profit when they offer the final product for a price that yields no such gain to less efficient suppliers. This condition must hold whether the more efficient supplier happens to be the landlord or the tenant.

We first will demonstrate the basic efficiency result using our hypothetical numerical example, and then we will show how to generalize it, indicating that the result is valid always, not just when the pertinent numbers happen in reality to match those in our illustration.

First, however, we must recall that even if every one of a firm's services is sold at a price equal to its average-incremental cost, the firm's total revenues may not cover its total costs. Consequently, it is normal and not anticompetitive for a firm to price some or all of its products to provide not only the required profit component of incremental cost, but also some contribution toward recovery of common fixed costs that do not enter the incremental costs of the individual products. The appropriate and viable size of the contribution of a particular product depends in part upon demand conditions for that product; it does not follow any standard markup rule or any arbitrary cost-allocation procedure. Any service whose price exceeds its per-unit incremental cost provides such a contribution in addition to the profit required on the incremental investment contained in the incremental cost.

With all this in mind, consider again our numerical example encompassing railroads X and Y. Suppose that the final product in question (transport from A to C) is sold to shippers at a price of $10 per ton—a price deemed competitive and thus above the incremental-cost floor. We have already assumed that landlord railroad X incurs an incremental cost for transport from A to B (which we will call IC_{AB}) that equals $3 per ton, and an incremental cost for transport from B to C (which we will call IC_{BXC}) that also equals $3 per ton. We saw that these incremental costs leave a net contribution toward common fixed costs of $4 per ton (that is, $10 - $3 - $3) from each unit of final product sold. And we saw that the efficient component-pricing principle requires that the landlord railroad X offer interconnection over route AB to tenant railroad Y at a price equal to IC_{AB} plus X's opportunity cost (that is, $3 + $4 = $7). At that price, the tenant's gross earnings per unit of final product amount to $3. This represents the $10 final-product price minus the $7 fee that the tenant pays to the landlord for interconnection over route AB. But to determine Y's *net* earnings we must also subtract from this sum the incremental cost tenant railroad Y incurs when it transports a ton of freight over its own route segment to complete the trip from A to C. There are three possibilities:

Case I: If tenant railroad Y is the less efficient supplier of the remainder of the final product (transport from B to C), so that its incremental cost (say, $4) exceeds the $3 incremental cost of landlord railroad X for transport from B to C, then Y will lose money if it attempts to provide the final product. Here, the $10 price for the final product must be exceeded by the $11 sum of the efficient component price ($7) plus Y's incremental cost of completing the final product, $4. So, Y will be kept out—not by an improper price, but because of its own inefficiency. That is the outcome required by the public interest.

Case II: If the incremental cost of providing transport from B to C is the same for both railroads ($3), then the two firms are equally efficient suppliers of transport from B to C. It does not matter to society which railroad provides the service. Moreover, the tenant will experience no gain and no loss by providing the service, since its profit in excess of incremental capital cost = price − trackage fee − Y's incremental cost over route BC = $10 − $7 − $3 = $0, so that the tenant, offered only a return equal to its capital cost, will be indifferent between entering and staying out.

Case III: In the third case, the tenant is the more efficient supplier of transport from B to C with an incremental cost of, say, $2. Y can then undercut slightly X's final-product price ($10) and make an additional profit for itself while still covering both the efficient component price that it must pay to X ($7) and its own incremental cost of completing the final product (which is less than $3). For example, Y can sell the final product for $9.75 per unit, making a profit of $0.75 per unit over the cost of capital (that is, $9.75 − $7 − $2). The landlord will have no incentive to retain for itself the transportation business from B to C. It could do so only by matching the tenant's $9.75 price. But at any price below $10 the landlord would be accepting a contribution less than the contribution ($4) that it can obtain through the efficient component prices it charges Y for Y's provision of transport from B to C.

In Case III above, the landlord is said to have chosen to "buy" rather than "make" the B-to-C transportation component of the final product. This result shows how the efficient component-pricing rule achieves the principle of indifference. That is, the rule sets the landlord's component price to include all its costs, so that the landlord is indifferent whether that particular transportation service is provided by itself or a rival, since all the landlord's costs are covered one way or the other. The rule thus ensures that the task of providing transport from B to C is performed by the firm that can do it more efficiently.

Matters work out differently if regulation forces the landlord to offer transport from A to B at a price *below* the efficient component price. If regulation permitted X, for example, to charge at most $5.50 for transport from A to B (rather than the $7 price permitted under the efficient component-pricing rule), then the tenant's gross earnings—that is, its final product price ($10) minus the rental price ($5.50)—would be $4.50, or $1.50 above X's incremental cost of providing transport from B to C. Even if Y's incremental cost of providing transport from B to C were $4, making it a *less* efficient supplier of the competitive transportation service than X, Y could still enter the arena and earn a contribution from its inefficient activity, for its per unit profit would then be $10 − $5.50 − $4 = $0.50. This profit to the less efficient supplier is made possible because the imposition of the $5.50 price offers the tenant a *subsidy* from the landlord of $1.50 for every unit of service the tenant elects to provide. Moreover, that subsidy is, in effect, obtainable by the tenant on demand, because the $5.50 price is imposed by the regulatory authority.

The connection between the efficient component-pricing rule and allocative efficiency should now be clear: the rule ensures proper pricing and efficiency in the competitive segment of the rail route, just as it will ensure this outcome in the local telecommunications loop. It only remains to be shown that the efficiency result is not unique to the numbers we happened to select for our illustration, but rather has general applicability. To show this, we now substitute algebraic symbols for the preceding numbers.

Formal Discussion of the Rule's Efficiency

A formal discussion enables us to prove the general efficiency of the component-pricing rule directly and offers some additional insights on its workings. In algebraic terms, the rule tells us that the appropriate per-train payment by the tenant railroad (the purchaser of access) Y is AIC, the per-unit incremental cost (excluding opportunity cost), plus T/M, where T was the total contribution to common fixed costs that X earned from the traffic over route AC before granting trackage rights, and M is the total number of trains (of both railroads together) going from A to C. First we prove that pricing in accord with the rule leaves the landlord indifferent between granting the trackage rights to the tenant and using the tracks for itself. Under the rule, the landlord railroad X will receive from Y, for Y's traffic consisting of N trains, a total payment equal to:

$$(N)(\text{AIC}) + NT/M, \tag{7.1}$$

giving X a contribution to profit equal to

$$(N)(\text{AIC}) + NT/M - \text{the cost to } X \text{ of } Y\text{'s traffic over } AB =$$

$$(N)(\text{AIC}) + NT/M - (N)(\text{AIC}) = NT/M. \tag{7.2}$$

This is the contribution X receives from Y's traffic. The contribution that X will receive from the $(M - N)$ trains of its own that continue to traverse the route after the grant of trackage rights will equal the number of its trains, $M - N$, multiplied by the contribution per train:

$$(M - N)\, T/M = T - NT/M. \tag{7.3}$$

So the landlord's gain from the combined traffic, after expending $(N)(\text{AIC})$ on Y's trains in the manner expressed in Equation (7.2), will be the sum of the contribution from Y's traffic given by Equation (7.2) and the contribution from its own traffic, Equation (7.3), that is

$$(NT/M) + T - NT/M = T. \tag{7.4}$$

In other words, under the optimal component-pricing rule, the landlord will gain the same total contribution T whether or not it grants the traffic rights, and despite the fact that the landlord now runs fewer trains of its own.[4] This outcome differs from the traditional regulatory arrangement, which assigns both X and Y a share of T, prorated in proportion to their respective shares—that is, $(M - N)$ and N, of the total traffic M.

Let us see now how this result relates to the issue of efficiency. Let AIC_X or AIC_Y be the per-train incremental cost if this competitive B-to-C portion of the transportation service is performed by X or Y, respectively. Then it will be more efficient for landlord railroad X to transport the freight if $AIC_X < AIC_Y$, and it will be more efficient for tenant railroad Y to do so if the inequality is reversed.[5]

To prove that the component-pricing rule automatically apportions the task to the more efficient carrier, we first provide an explicit expression for the contribution T of the total traffic over route AC. For this purpose, let P represent the price that shippers pay to transport an entire trainload of freight over the entire route AC. Then, in the absence of its grant of trackage rights to Y, X obtains from its train traffic M the following contribution:

$$T = M(P - \text{AIC} - \text{AIC}_X), \tag{7.5}$$

4. The efficient component-pricing rule may appear, therefore, to conflict with the result contributed by Peter A. Diamond & John A. Mirrlees, *Optimal Taxation and Public Production, II: Tax Rules*, 61 AM. ECON. REV. 261 (1971), which asserts that in a Ramsey solution it is inefficient for the price of any intermediate good to include any markup over marginal cost. There is no such conflict here, however, since true marginal cost must include all of the (social) marginal opportunity cost. The contribution derived from the tenant by the landlord is simply part of the landlord's opportunity cost incurred in providing trackage space to the tenant: the contribution entails no Ramsey markup over *that* marginal cost.

It should be noted, incidentally, that as is usual in discussions of Ramsey analysis, Diamond and Mirrlees do not consider cases of scale economies, so that the allocation of production among firms entails an interior maximum in whose determination MC rather than AIC plays the key cost role.

5. It is easy to extend the analysis to the case where efficiency requires each railroad to carry part of the traffic, apportioned so that $MC_X = MC_Y$, where MC_X is the marginal cost to railroad X of carrying an additional unit (carload or ton) of freight over route segment BC.

where AIC is, as before, the incremental cost of taking a train over the noncompetitive route segment *AB*, and AIC_X is *X*'s incremental cost of carrying the train the remainder of the way over route *BXC*. Now, if *Y* acquires trackage rights and sends *N* trains from *A* to *C*, it will earn a profit equal to its total revenue *PN*, minus its optimal input-price payment given by Equation (7.1), minus $(N)(\text{AIC}_Y)$, the incremental cost it incurs by carrying the *N* trains over its own route *BYC*. That is,

$$Y\text{'s profit} = N(P - \text{AIC} - T/M - \text{AIC}_Y), \tag{7.6}$$

or, substituting the value of *T/M* obtainable from Equation (7.5),

$$Y\text{'s profit} = N(P - \text{AIC} - P + \text{AIC} + \text{AIC}_X - \text{AIC}_Y)$$

$$= N(\text{AIC}_X - \text{AIC}_Y). \tag{7.7}$$

Thus *Y* will profit by renting the trackage rights from *X* if and only if *Y* is the more efficient carrier, so that $\text{AIC}_Y < \text{AIC}_X$. Indeed, *Y*'s profit will then equal the net resources that society saves by use of *Y* rather than *X*. Equation (7.7) also shows that, when the pricing of the trackage rights follows the efficient component-pricing rule, *Y* will lose money by acquiring those rights if it is the less efficient carrier.

In sum, in its allocation of the traffic between *X* and *Y*, the rent-setting rule presented in Equation (7.1) is, indeed, optimal.[6] The same logic applies without modification to the pricing of access to the local telecommunications loop.

---

6. Those who consider it inequitable for the landlord to be paid the full opportunity cost of its rental have referred to such pricing as "a perfect price squeeze." *See, e.g.,* WILLIAM B. TYE, THE THEORY OF CONTESTABLE MARKETS: APPLICATIONS TO REGULATORY AND ANTITRUST PROBLEMS IN THE RAIL INDUSTRY 65–69 (Greenwood Press 1990). Equation (7.7) shows, however, that the efficient component-pricing rule gives the tenant all the fruits of whatever superiority in efficiency it may provide.

*Controversial Components of Opportunity Cost: Loss of Monopoly
Markup and Special-Service Obligations*

Often it is objected that the efficient component-pricing rule is a means
to ensure that the landlord can continue receiving any monopoly profits
it has been able to earn on the final product. Suppose that, in the absence of the tenant, the landlord has monopoly power in the final-product market and earns a high rate of profit on sales. If, by supplying the
input to the tenant, the landlord permits the tenant to take away some
of those profitable sales, then the monopoly profit on those forgone
final-product sales is indeed an opportunity cost to the landlord. According to the optimal input-pricing rule, the tenant should be required
to compensate the landlord for that loss. This ensures the monopoly
earnings to the landlord and undercuts the tenant's power to introduce
effective competition into the final-product market and thereby to reduce prices to their competitive levels.

All this is true, but the villain of the piece is not the optimal input-
pricing rule. The real problem is that the landlord has been permitted
to charge monopoly prices for the final product in the first place. Had
the stand-alone-cost ceiling upon final-product prices been enforced,
the landlord could never have earned the monopoly profit in this
regulatory scenario. Thus, the error is the failure to impose the stand-
alone-cost ceiling on the final-product price, not the use of the optimal
input-pricing rule. As we explained earlier, the regulatory rules
described in this monograph will do their full job only if they are all
carried out together. Partial adoption or enforcement of the rules will
not achieve all the desired results.

A related issue arises when a regulated firm has special-service
obligations imposed upon it. Examples include the arrangement under
which the input supplier is also forced to serve as the "carrier of last
resort," or when, as in the case of Telecom Corporation of New Zealand, the carrier is required to supply services to residential customers
at rates that it claims to be insufficient to cover the pertinent incremental costs.[7] These obligations are appropriately treated as sources of

---

7. Clear Communications, Ltd. *v.* Telecom Corp. of New Zealand, Ltd., slip op. (H.C.
Dec. 22, 1992).

common fixed costs for the firm; the costs must be covered legitimately by the firm's prices and be taken into account in calculating its stand-alone-cost ceilings.

Here the hypothetical entrant, whose costs constitute the stand-alone-cost ceiling, should have imposed upon it the same special-service obligations as those borne by the incumbent. To do otherwise is to condemn the regulated firm to incur losses. In any competitive market equilibrium where costs are imposed by fiat upon all firms and prospective entrants, prices will have to cover those costs in addition to any other costs of the efficient suppliers. In that case, the opportunity cost when sales are lost because of the supply of an input to a competitor must also make up for any forgone contribution to coverage of the costs of special-service obligations imposed by regulators. But if those costs are imposed on only one firm, with current rivals and entrants exempted, a special handicap is clearly borne by that firm and competition will prevent it from recovering those costs.

Opportunity Costs, Network Externalities, and Demand Complementarities

Another bit of clarification is required here. The preceding discussion should not be interpreted to imply that when access provided by a LEC to, say, an IXC leads to the sale of an additional X message minutes of business by the IXC along a given intraLATA route, the result will necessarily be an equal loss of business by the LEC. For simplicity of exposition, we have used in the preceding text the case of the zero-sum game—whatever business an entrant gains is business lost by the incumbent. To be sure, markets do not necessarily work that way in reality. Entrants are known to beat the bushes for customers who were not previous users of the product in question. Moreover, there is evidence indicating that the two-way nature of telecommunications produces a beneficial *network externality*: an individual consumer's demand for use of the network increases with the number of other users on the network.[8] Thus, if the entrant brings in some new customers, it can

---

8. *See, e.g.*, BRIDGER M. MITCHELL & INGO VOGELSANG, TELECOMMUNICATIONS

to some degree stimulate demand for the incumbent's services. In addition to the presence of such network externalities, the LEC's supply of access to a competitor can conceivably stimulate demand for the LEC's final product if there is complementarity of the two demands associated with the volume of traffic—for example, more household traffic can stimulate business telephone usage.[9]

Thus, an entering IXC is likely to devote effort to expanding the market, using the access to serve at least some new business that entails no reduction in LEC volume and can, possibly, bring a bit of additional traffic to the LEC. In that case, the pertinent opportunity cost to the LEC of the supply of access will be lower than if the added IXC volume is added directly and fully at the expense of LEC sales. The pertinent opportunity-cost figure is, of course, the contribution actually forgone by the LEC, not the contribution it would have lost if all of the IXC's gain had come at the LEC's expense.

Explicit Access Charges to the IXC and Implicit Access Charges of the LEC to Itself

The efficient component-pricing rule has two important applications to the regulation of local telephone service. First, it tells us what price it is appropriate for the LEC to charge the IXCs for access service. More generally, it indicates the price that any other variety of competitor of the LEC should pay to receive the necessary access to the local loop.

Second, the analysis underlying the rule indicates how the LEC should price the *final product*, intraLATA toll service, when selling that product to consumers. As we see next, the LEC's production of

---

PRICING: THEORY AND PRACTICE 11 (Cambridge Univ. Press 1991); JEAN TIROLE, THE THEORY OF INDUSTRIAL ORGANIZATION 405 (MIT Press 1988). Usually, we think of the network externality in telecommunications accruing when another access line or another node (exchange) is added to the network. "When a new node is added, the externality is reflected in the number of calls made between any existing nodes and the new node (not an increase in the calls between existing nodes)." MITCHELL & VOGELSANG, *supra*, at 11.

9. A forthcoming book estimates the empirical magnitudes of such complementarity effects in telecommunications demand. *See* LESTER D. TAYLOR, TELECOMMUNICATIONS DEMAND (Kluwer Academic Publishers forthcoming 1993).

that service, too, entails an opportunity cost for itself. Hence, the price of that final product must at least equal its average-incremental cost, including the pertinent opportunity cost.

The opportunity cost to the LEC of the LEC's own final-product sales is determined by the price the LEC charges IXCs for access—a price governed by the optimal input-pricing rule. The LEC, in effect, must choose between supplying access to the final consumer directly or selling the access to an IXC, which would provide the final product—intraLATA toll service—to that same consumer. Either action requires that the other sale be forgone. The sale of the final product by the LEC to a telecommunications consumer enables the LEC to supply the final product—but it could otherwise have been provided by an IXC, which would have had to purchase access service from the LEC. Thus, the sale of the final product by the LEC entails a forgone access profit. The magnitude of this forgone profit, or opportunity cost, is determined by the price of the sale of access to the IXC, as governed by the optimal input-pricing rule. But we have proved, earlier in this chapter, that when the access price follows the input-pricing rule the LEC must receive exactly the same profit, whether it uses the access service itself or sells it to an IXC. That is the parity principle that enables the more efficient supplier to win out.

The cliché used to describe this objective of the optimal input-pricing exercise is to ensure a "level playing field" for the competitive efforts of the IXCs and the LEC. When access, priced by the rule, is used by either a LEC or an IXC to provide the final product to consumers, it will still be possible for one of the suppliers to undercut the final-product price of the other, but only if that supplier is the more efficient provider. That is so because the more efficient supplier will incur lower direct incremental costs, even though its final-product prices are not allowed to contribute less profit to the supply of access. By ensuring that the implicit price of access by the LEC to itself and the explicit price to the IXC are the same, the playing field in the sale of final-product telecommunications services is truly leveled.

Use of the optimal component-pricing rule sometimes has been complicated in practice. Institutional arrangements can create an artificial asymmetry between the contribution forgone by the supplier of the inputs when it sacrifices sales of the input to a competing supplier of the final product and the contribution forgone when it sacrifices sales of the input to one of its own customers in the market for the final product. In one case, the local telephone company is constrained, by a combination of past practice and regulation, to use one set of facilities, A, in supplying access to the interexchange carriers, and another set of facilities, B, in supplying interconnection for its own toll calls into the local loop. Under current pricing arrangements, the LEC receives a larger contribution from a message using B than from one employing A. Consequently, the opportunity cost when the LEC provides interconnection to itself instead of an IXC is different from the opportunity cost incurred when the LEC supplies interconnection to the IXC rather than itself. In this case, the supply of interconnection for an IXC call, which is presumed to deprive the local exchange carrier of that item of final-product business, entails a larger opportunity cost than does the opposite process—namely, the use of the facilities by the LEC to provide the final product to its own customers.

The danger here is that the LEC will use this asymmetry of opportunity costs to bias market conditions in its own favor, charging the IXC more for interconnection to the local loop than it implicitly charges itself for the same service. The problem lies not in recognizing the appropriate role of opportunity cost in pricing, but in the pricing arrangement that yields different profits to two different processes supplying the same service. Clearly, that outcome violates the dictates of the competitive-market standard, which would soon bring profits from the use of the A access facilities into line with those from the B interconnection facilities. In a fully competitive market, either entry would quickly erode the profits from the more lucrative facilities toward the level of profits offered by the other facilities, or the less profitable facilities would soon be abandoned.

Thus, where this situation of asymmetric opportunity costs arises, the regulator should require, or at least provide, strong incentives for equalization of the contributions offered by the two sets of facilities. This problem is no reason to abandon the efficient component-pricing rule, or to acquiesce to biasing input pricing in favor of one affected party.

Marginal and Inframarginal Opportunity Cost

The subject of opportunity cost involves a subtle technical complication, evidently unrecognized in much of the economic literature, that can be of considerable importance in particular cases. In some circumstances total opportunity costs, even though substantial, can be close to zero at the margin. The marginal opportunity cost of the sale or lease of some good or service can clearly be positive if the item is limited in supply or entails some fixed capacity, so that the more the seller supplies to others, the less it has available for its own use. A firm that lets others use a bridge whose capacity was already fully employed to transport its own products obviously is apt to incur an opportunity cost even when it permits just one additional person to cross.

But if a LEC can easily expand the facilities it uses to provide access, then its sale of access to others does not entail any such capacity limitation. In general, if a product supplier can expand capacity and is prepared to do so until the marginal profit of further additions to capacity is zero, then no corresponding *marginal* opportunity cost in the sale of the product will arise from a resulting unavailability of capacity to the seller.

The same can be true of an opportunity cost that arises when the recipient of access (or some other input) uses it to take profitable business away from the input supplier. It can be argued that if a firm is a profit-maximizer, then each of its activities will be carried to the point where it yields zero economic profit at the margin. Thus the opportunity cost of losing the marginal unit of any product of one of its activities can be expected to disappear. This valid observation has been used to argue that while price floors for final products as well as the optimal input prices should all include opportunity costs, if there are any, in practice this can often be ignored because at least marginal opportunity costs are frequently zero.

This argument is misleading, however, because it fails to consider the pertinent margin. If the price of access is set so low that an IXC can take away a high proportion of the sales of intraLATA long-distance service by the LEC, then *much* more than the zero-profit marginal unit of the LEC's original sales volume will be lost. That is, the IXC is virtually certain to wrest away a substantial increment of the

LEC's business, not just a single, marginal unit. Then, the remaining business can easily offer far more than a zero marginal profit, because output will have been cut from the precompetition profit-maximizing level. Hence, a substantial opportunity cost can be borne by the LEC on the margin if, having permitted substantial incursions into its business by an IXC, it permits the IXC to sell still another unit of the product at the new output level. This is the fuller implication of the IXC's marginal use of access.

Scale economies present yet another reason why the opportunity cost incurred by supplying access to a rival can substantially affect the efficient price for use of that input and cannot simply be ignored. As has been shown, where production of the particular commodity is characterized by scale economies, average-incremental cost replaces marginal cost as the pertinent standard for final-product prices consistent with efficiency in production. Efficiency in production then requires that where the product is characterized by declining average-incremental cost, price be set no lower than average-incremental cost.

The role of average-incremental cost in regulating the price of a homogeneous service is pertinent to the issue we have just been discussing—the role of opportunity cost in determining the efficient price. We have just noted that sometimes, particularly when opportunity cost is not created by capacity limitations, marginal opportunity cost can be driven to zero. This is possible when the supplier of the facility can expand capacity to the point that enables him to use as much as he wants for his own purposes and to sell or lease as much capacity to others as he desires.

But in such a case, even though *marginal* opportunity cost may be zero because capacity will be expanded by a profit-maximizing firm to the point where the enterprise gains nothing by adding yet another unit, it does not follow that the opportunity cost on *inframarginal* units of capacity will also be zero. If inframarginal units do yield positive benefits to the owner when used for his own purposes, and if some substantial proportion of that capacity is nevertheless rented or sold to someone else, then that transaction will clearly entail a nonzero opportunity cost—the sum of the forgone inframarginal benefits. That is, the average-incremental opportunity cost will be positive; the efficient price, which should at least equal AIC, must cover the nonzero opportunity-cost component as well.

Entry by Efficient Rivals

A final word is necessary on the pertinence of the efficient component-pricing rule to the opportunity for entry. In a competitive market, an incumbent will levy on a new entrant an access charge that will cover both the direct incremental cost of providing the access and its opportunity cost. As we have seen, the latter represents the contribution of the access-using service either toward meeting a shortfall in the price of another service and/or toward recovery of the common fixed costs of supplying some or all of the incumbent's services. An access charge large enough for these purposes may at first glance seem to constitute an inappropriate competitive disadvantage to the entrant, since it requires the entrant to make such a contribution even though the incumbent may not be performing these activities efficiently, and the entrant itself may have to undertake similar activities to support its own services.

Closer inspection, however, confirms that these impressions are mistaken. As we have shown, the efficient component-pricing rule offers the prospect of success to entrants who can add efficiency to the supply of the final product, while it ensures that inefficient entrants are not made profitable by an implicit cross-subsidy extracted from the incumbent. An entrant may have to replicate some of the incumbent's activities or facilities, and the costs of such duplication can render an entrant unprofitable. But if that is the case under efficient component pricing, then the requisite replication of costs correspondingly renders the entry inefficient and, ultimately, harmful to consumers and to society.

This is exactly what occurs in an ideally competitive or contestable market. After all, one of the chief benefits of competitive markets is their intolerance of inefficient supply arrangements. Input pricing that discourages inefficient entry cannot be said to constitute an undue competitive disadvantage, any more than the efficient workings of competitive markets can be labeled anticompetitive, even if they lead to the demise of less efficient firms.

Conclusion

This completes our analysis of the efficient component-pricing rule for the pricing of access or any other input used both by the input producer and by competitors in supplying final products. Using a railroading analogy, we showed how the optimal rental fee for access to a monopolist's tracks is the sum of the direct incremental cost of permitting the tenant railroad to use the tracks and the opportunity cost to the landlord railroad of supplying this downstream competitor with access to those tracks. The trackage-rights problem is perfectly analogous to the LEC's supply of access to IXCs, and to myriad situations in network industries in which one firm produces an intermediate good—access to the network—that constitutes a necessary input for its competitors in the market for the final product sold to consumers.

The working of the efficient component-pricing rule is perfectly general. The rule *always* assigns the supplier's task to the firm that can do it most efficiently. A price lower than that set in accordance with the rule—as seems often to have happened under regulatory decisions on the division of profit between the input producer and the final product supplier—always constitutes an interfirm cross-subsidy and so invites the assumption of the supplier's role by a firm that is not the most efficient provider. This result should not come as a surprise. It is well known that economic forces set component prices in competitive markets in this way, and competitive market prices are generally those necessary to achieve economic efficiency. Thus, our efficiency result also follows immediately through this indirect route, using the competitive-market standard as the guide to efficient pricing.

8

Policies to Promote Entry

THE EFFECTIVENESS OF COMPETITION in local telecommunications is currently under debate. Natural impediments inherent in the older technology still inhibit the entry of interexchange carriers into the local telephone arena, and restrictions in the MFJ prevent some local exchange carriers from entering certain interexchange activities. As was described in some detail in Chapter 2, however, some entry into strictly local services is already under way, with the aid of wireless techniques—which in the long run may prove the more effective form of transport for much of local traffic. Any prohibitions against IXC entry, and any prevention of entry by the LECs and the cable companies into one another's territory, will postpone the fruits of competition. If regulatory impediments are removed, entry may well occur rapidly and substantially in at least some of the telecommunications markets currently operated as monopolies. The question is on what terms such entry should be permitted, and whether there is ever any reason to prevent it.

Policies Concerning Entry into Local Telecommunications

There would appear to be little reason to continue current entry restrictions. The current regulatory regime, in effect, undertakes to defend the public interest through the formation and careful enforcement of an extensive cartel arrangement. This arrangement divides the markets of the interrelated subindustries at issue, assigning to each its own terrain, which is meticulously monitored against incursions by any other type of enterprise.[1]

It seems absurd to believe that the general welfare will be promoted by such an arrangement. The public interest never gains by preventing competition, by granting special protection to shaky enterprises such as financially troubled newspapers, or by shielding firms against the competition of more effective rivals who threaten to succeed through lower costs or superior products. Thus the public has little to gain and much to lose from statutes, regulations, and consent decrees that, to take a salient example, exclude cable television carriers from local telephone services and exclude the LECs from providing television programming and information services.

But what about the danger of cross-subsidy and predatory pricing if firms that arguably possess bottleneck facilities are permitted to invade the fields of other enterprises? Some lawyers and economists, particularly those associated with the Chicago School of antitrust analysis, believe that the danger of these practices occurring in unregulated markets with any noteworthy frequency has been exaggerated.[2] Even Professors Areeda and Turner admit that "proven cases of predatory pricing have been extremely rare."[3] Similarly, and perhaps not surprisingly, in recent years the Supreme Court has repeatedly expressed skepticism about the plausibility of charges of predation.[4] Other law-

---

1. *See, e.g.*, Robert W. Crandall, *Regulating Communications: Creating Monopoly While "Protecting" Us From It*, BROOKINGS REV., vol. 10, no. 3, at 29 (Summer 1992).

2. *See, e.g.*, ROBERT H. BORK, THE ANTITRUST PARADOX: A POLICY AT WAR WITH ITSELF 144–59 (Free Press rev. ed. 1993); YALE BROZEN, CONCENTRATION, MERGERS, AND PUBLIC POLICY 163, 392 (Macmillan Publishing Co. 1982); RICHARD A. POSNER, ANTITRUST LAW: AN ECONOMIC PERSPECTIVE 184–96 (Univ. of Chicago Press 1976); J. Gregory Sidak, *Debunking Predatory Innovation*, 83 COLUM. L. REV. 1121 (1983); Frank H. Easterbrook, *Predatory Strategies and Counterstrategies*, 48 U. CHI. L. REV. 263 (1981). *See also* A.A. Poultry Farms, Inc. *v.* Rose Acre Farms, Inc., 881 F.2d 1396, 1401 (7th Cir. 1989) (Easterbrook, J.), *cert. denied*, 494 U.S. 1019 (1990).

3. Phillip Areeda & Donald F. Turner, *Predatory Pricing and Related Practices Under Section 2 of the Sherman Act*, 88 HARV. L. REV. 699, 718 (1975), *quoted in* BROZEN, *supra* note 2, at 163.

4. Brooke Group Ltd. *v.* Brown & Williamson Tobacco Corp., 113 S. Ct. 2578 (1993); Atlantic Richfield Co. *v.* USA Petroleum Co., 495 U.S. 328, 340 (1990); Matsushita Elec. Indus. Co. *v.* Zenith Radio Corp., 475 U.S. 574, 589 (1986).

yers and economists, however, argue that predatory pricing can be rational under certain conditions and that this view is supported by new insights from game theory, so that predatory pricing may constitute a legitimate concern even in unregulated markets.[5]

One need not resolve this debate over predatory pricing in general to conclude that extended freedom of entry is desirable in telecommunications. The regulatory regime that we have described in these pages is designed to deal with precisely this issue. These rules are increasingly attractive to state regulators and legislatures, so their adoption is becoming reality.

An admirable example of real-world adoption of these rules is the Illinois statute enacted in 1992.[6] It represents desirable public policy in accordance with the criteria we have proposed here because it fosters competition while adopting rational principles to regulate the LECs. The statute requires LECs to calculate long-run incremental cost for the entire service and for appropriate groups of services.[7] It calls for imputation—that is, the adoption of the efficient component-pricing rule.[8] It requires unbundling, and nondiscriminatory provision and pricing of the unbundled services.[9] It also avoids prohibition of interconnection and the imposition of monopoly franchising of local facilities, leaving the Illinois Commerce Commission free to act on these two matters.[10]

If prices of services in which market power persists, or is merely feared to persist, are constrained by the rules that we have described here and that are already embodied in some regulatory regimes, neither cross-subsidy nor predatory pricing should be possible. Of course, if entry is permitted under such a regulatory regime, and if competition establishes itself firmly, it will eventually become desirable to remove

---

5. *See* Alvin K. Klevorick, *The Current State of the Law and Economics of Predatory Pricing,* 83 AM. ECON. REV. PAPERS & PROC. 162 (1993) (surveying recent economic literature).

6. Ill. Pub. Act 87-895 (codified at ILL. REV. STAT. ch. 220, § 13-505.1 *et seq.* (1993)).

7. ILL. REV. STAT. ch. 220, § 13-505.1 (1993).

8. *Id.*

9. *Id.* §§ 13-505.2, 13-505.6.

10. *Id.* §§ 13-505.4, 13-505.5.

these rules will become superfluous. But until then, the rules should ensure that market power is not exercised by entrants making incursions into rivals' territories for the purpose of destroying or inhibiting true competition.

Governmental restrictions upon entry may bear prime responsibility for any continued ability on the part of the LECs to use cross-subsidy as an anticompetitive device. Such restrictions probably bear much of the responsibility for whatever market power the LECs continue to possess—the only power that can make possible continued cross-subsidy of the sort desired by regulators. If so, then elimination of governmentally imposed barriers to entry may prove to be the most potent preventative of the very cross-subsidies held to be the strongest argument against deregulation.

Natural Monopoly and the Market Test

Whether or not rivals enter the most crucial telephone services arena on a substantial scale—and if so, whether they succeed—will depend on both the regulatory rules and the underlying economic circumstances. Entry cannot be expected to succeed in a market that qualifies as a natural monopoly—that is, a market whose bundle of goods and services can be provided more cheaply by a single enterprise than by any combination of smaller or more specialized firms. If an activity is characterized by economies of scale, then a single large enterprise can always earn a competitive profit and yet undercut any set of smaller rivals together supplying the same bundle of outputs.

A similar conclusion follows if an activity is characterized by economies of scope, whereby a single firm saves money by supplying many or all the goods and services that its activity can yield, in comparison with the outlays incurred by a set of more specialized firms, each of which supplies only a few of the products. Where an industry is a natural monopoly, a multiplicity of smaller, more specialized firms generally cannot survive, or they can survive only with the aid of subsidy. Since a larger firm incurs lower costs, the smaller firms cannot match the prices of the larger firm without encountering financial difficulties. Nor does it serve the public interest for a multiplicity of firms to continue operating in a natural monopoly arena. Their survival will waste resources of society, and it can be ensured only by charging prices sufficiently high to cover the costs incurred through their small-scale operation. In such an arena, competition can survive only at the expense of the consumer, a doubtful blessing to the public interest.

Since we cannot be certain which arenas of local telephone service, if any, are natural monopolies, it would be senseless for the regulator to try to determine which areas have this attribute and to permit entry into only those sectors deemed not to be natural monopolies. Rather, the most rational way to distinguish the arenas into which entry is feasible is to let the market decide. This can be done by opening *all* local telecommunications to entry, imposing some rules to guard against the erection or perpetuation of artificial barriers to entry, and then observing where entry prospers and where it does not. The former will then be the naturally competitive fields, the latter the natural monopolies.

Rules Against Erecting Barriers to Entry

Competition has become possible in areas of local telephony where it could not arise before. Where this is so, there is reason to reduce or eliminate regulatory intervention. Yet changes will be necessary in current arrangements for interconnection, bundling, and pricing of access for deregulation to be efficacious.

Under what rules will deregulation of particular local activities not confer the freedom to exercise market power but, rather, ensure that the market test is executed without interference? What rules, in other words, must the regulator adopt to ensure that no artificial barriers to entry are constructed? A few simple provisions would appear to suffice:

1. Supply of interconnection should be required for all qualified applicants. That is, any telecommunications firm that demands a service such as access should be guaranteed it. Such interconnection should include transport activities. In addition, it should be available

for each of the basic network functions (BNFs) that the LEC can supply to itself. These BNFs include use of the loops, switches, and signaling, as well as transport. Such interconnection will encourage specialized, but prospectively significant, forms of competition; it will preclude objectionable tying arrangements that can possibly prevent a prospective competitor from seeking to serve a LEC customer.

2. Thus, the LEC networks should comprehensively unbundle the BNFs, each of which should be offered separately for sale at prices based on costs. That is, any other telecommunications firm that wants interconnection for a particular service it supplies—particularly one supplied in competition with the LEC—must not be denied interconnection for that service alone. Nor may such a firm be charged a particularly high price for that interconnection unless it is purchased along with other services supplied by the LEC (bundling). Some argue that the basic network functions rather than the LEC services constitute remaining bottlenecks. When the BNFs are offered to all who want to use them at appropriate prices, and when the LECs' competitors take advantage of the offer, it will be clear that those bottlenecks have disappeared.

3. The interconnection service should be supplied on identical technical and quality terms to all who want to purchase it. The LEC, however, should be allowed to offer all customers a choice between higher- and lower-quality interconnection at suitable prices.

4. The pricing of interconnection should be governed by the efficient component-pricing rule, to ensure that competition is not undermined by input-price discrimination, including discrimination by the LEC in its own favor.

5. Restrictions on resale and user restrictions should be terminated, in order to facilitate the spread of competitive pressures and to provide full freedom for competitors and prospective competitors to assemble attractive service offerings.

6. The price floors for final products described in Chapter 4 must be enforced to prevent cross-subsidy and predatory pricing.

7. Steps should be taken to ensure that telephone-number assignment is carried out without favoring any particular party, and that number portability is not impeded.[11]

8. Franchising restrictions, which are direct impediments to entry, should be eliminated. In light of the convergence between local telephony and cable television, it should be clear that the same rule against exclusive franchising—*de jure* or *de facto*—should be adopted in the latter industry.[12]

9. The FCC should expeditiously allocate spectrum for personal communications services and other forms of wireless technology that promise to increase competition for local access and transport.[13]

10. The regulatory agency must discourage legal actions that are without merit, and whose only purpose is to harass actual or potential competitors or to prevent effective competitive acts by rivals.[14]

---

11. *Cf.* Provision of Access for 800 Service, Mem. Op. & Order on Further Recon., CC Dkt. No. 86-10, 8 F.C.C. Rec. 1038 (1993); Competition in the Interstate Interexchange Marketplace, Rep. & Order, CC Dkt. No. 90-132, 6 F.C.C. Rec. 5880, 5904 ¶¶ 138–40 (1991).

12. It is therefore laudable that the Cable Television Consumer Protection and Competition Act of 1992 provides that "a franchising authority may not grant an exclusive franchise and may not unreasonably refuse to award an additional competitive franchise." Pub. L. No. 102-385, § 7, 106 Stat. 1460, 1483 (1992) (amending 47 U.S.C. § 541(a)(1)). On the cost to consumers of exclusive franchising in cable television, see Thomas W. Hazlett, *The Demand to Regulate Franchise Monopoly: Evidence from CATV Rate Deregulation in California*, 29 ECON. INQUIRY 275 (1991); Thomas W. Hazlett, *Duopolistic Competition in CATV: Implications for Public Policy*, 7 YALE J. ON REG. 65 (1990); Thomas W. Hazlett, *Private Monopoly and the Public Interest: An Economic Analysis of the Cable Television Franchise*, 134 U. PA. L. REV. 1335 (1986).

13. *See* GEORGE CALHOUN, WIRELESS ACCESS AND THE LOCAL TELEPHONE NETWORK 568-71 (Artech House, Inc. 1992).

14. This task may prove difficult in view of the Supreme Court's recent holding that litigation undertaken to hinder a competitor is immune, by virtue of the First Amendment, from antitrust liability unless it can be shown to be "objectively baseless

The purpose of the ten preceding rules is obvious, except for the second rule, which was not discussed previously.

Unbundling Basic Network Functions

The unbundling problem arises when a prospective rival to the LEC wants to enter the market, but hopes to do so by offering only a few specialized services. The problem can arise also when a current competitor of the LEC undertakes by contract to provide only a few specialized services to a particular large customer. The LEC can prevent such specialized services from being offered by refusing to provide interconnection for them alone, or by charging a prohibitive price for such interconnection unless purchased as part of a bundle of services, many of which are not necessary to the buyer.

The possible problems associated with bundling can be prevented by requiring the LEC to provide interconnection for any of services or BNFs $A, B, C, \ldots$, either individually or together, as the customer desires, with the sum of the prices charged for each service equal to the price of the bundle—except to the extent that economies of scope are lost by providing the interconnection services individually rather than in a bundle. Of course, one cannot judge in the abstract whether such economies of scope are rare or common. Obviously, where such a loss of economies occurs, it is proper for the sum of the prices of the single-product interconnections to exceed the price of the bundle by the value of the economies of scope forgone by unbundled sales.

It is not obvious which of the parties in a dispute on such matters is best required to bear the evidentiary burden of proving the presence or absence of economies of scope. It seems plausible that the LECs, as the suppliers of the services and of the actual operators of the technology, are better positioned to do so. With these few rules, artificial barriers to entry will not arise, and the market test will be effective in directing entry where it will contribute to the general welfare.

in the sense that no reasonable litigant could realistically expect success on the merits." Professional Real Estate Investors, Inc. *v.* Columbia Pictures, 113 S. Ct. 1920, 1928 (1993).

The Special Problem of IntraLATA Toll Competition

One arena in which barriers to entry erected by regulation have proved peculiarly resistant to erosion is intraLATA toll service. In the MFJ, the regions assigned to the LECs were subdivided into smaller local access and transport areas, or LATAs. These include the local loops, but they also encompass some toll services, consisting of intrastate, and in some cases interstate, long-distance services. Ever since adoption of the MFJ, the interexchange carriers have sought permission to enter the intrastate portions of this arena. They have argued that there is considerable prospective demand for their provision of this service, both by business customers and by many of their household subscribers. In addition, on the production side, because the IXCs' networks are not designed in a manner consistent with LATA boundaries, it is inefficient and unnatural to truncate at the LATA borders the activities of the IXCs—or, for that matter, those of the LECs, once they have shed any significant vestige of market power.

Yet the LECs, resisting competition from this quarter as from others, have sought to prevent the entry of the IXCs into intraLATA toll service. They have argued that such competition would make it difficult to preserve intraLATA toll charges as a source of cross-subsidy to keep rates for local telephone service low and, correspondingly, to promote the regulatory goal of universal service—that is, effectively 100 percent household subscription to telephone service. Many regulators seem persuaded by this argument, as a number of states still have not permitted the IXCs to enter intraLATA toll service.[15] Even where such entry has been allowed, access by a caller to IXC service requires the dialing of five additional numbers beyond those needed to

---

15. *See* NATIONAL ASSOCIATION OF REGULATORY UTILITY COMMISSIONERS, THE STATUS OF COMPETITION IN INTRASTATE TELECOMMUNICATIONS (1992). The precise number of states that prevent IXC entry into intraLATA toll service depends on how one defines entry. As of August 1992, NARUC reported that thirteen states did not permit facilities-based competition in intraLATA toll service: Arkansas, Georgia, Hawaii, Kansas, Montana, Nevada, New Hampshire, New Jersey, New Mexico, Oklahoma, Rhode Island, Utah, and Wisconsin. *Id.* In addition, four states—Arizona, Hawaii, Nevada, and Rhode Island—did not permit competition in that market through resale. *Id.* Some of the thirty-seven states that do permit IXC entry into the intraLATA toll market nonetheless impose regulatory burdens on these entrants, such as restrictions on advertising. *Id.*

obtain the service provided by the LEC. As a result of this disparity, presumably, the IXCs have been able to acquire only insignificant market shares.

It is questionable whether IXC entry into the intraLATA toll arena will raise local rates. The rise in IXC business resulting from full and free entry is likely to increase the IXCs' total access-charge payments to the LECs, especially if competition reduces intraLATA toll charges and thus stimulates the volume of traffic in that arena. Recent econometric evidence indicates that IXC entry in states where it is permitted has caused no statistically significant rise in local telephone rates, either relative to states in which such entry is prohibited or relative to past trends in prices for local services.[16] Of course, matters may change as new technology makes it easier for the IXCs to bypass the LECs' facilities in the origination and termination of toll calls. The presence of the wireless and fiber services and, prospectively, of the "cable telephony" companies may modify the state of affairs drastically, forcing access rates down and reducing their ability to subsidize residential service.

In any event, the argument favoring this cross-subsidy is unlikely to persuade an economist. This is particularly so, given the empirical evidence suggesting that low-income household subscribers are not relatively lower users of long-distance services than are wealthier subscribers. Thus, one cannot justify opposing a reduction in the prices of such services, offset by a rise in local-service prices, by claiming that it would favor the rich over the poor.[17]

Moreover, if competition benefits virtually all subscribers, it is difficult to defend preservation of a monopoly in the intraLATA toll arena by regulatory fiat. It is improbable that this arena is a natural monopoly. Even if some claim it is so, they cannot reasonably object to letting the market decide the issue.

16. DAVID L. KASERMAN, JOHN W. MAYO, LARRY BLANK & SIMRAN KAHAI, OPEN ENTRY AND LOCAL TELEPHONE RATES: THE ECONOMICS OF INTRALATA TOLL COMPETITION (Univ. of Tennessee working paper 1993).

17. *See* ROBERT W. CRANDALL, AFTER THE BREAKUP: U.S. TELECOMMUNICATIONS IN A MORE COMPETITIVE ERA 107–15 (Brookings Institution 1991).

Public Intervention to Assist the Entrant

Given the likelihood that entry by new but substantial firms into local telephone service will soon occur, it is useful to review pertinent regulatory developments that occurred in the wake of entry into other arenas previously served by a regulated or a nationalized monopoly. These experiences, and some of the questionable policies they brought with them, may help to prevent similar mistakes from being made in local telephone service.

A paradox has characterized the behavior of almost all regulatory agencies on such occasions. In earlier periods, the regulator resisted entry with determination. Entry was considered permissible only upon presentation of weighty evidence of its redeeming social value—that it was required by "public convenience and necessity."[18] But then the regulatory agency's sympathies swung to the opposite extreme, and it became determined to protect entrants from danger, no matter what the cost to the public. More than one regulatory agency has done so quite openly, subjecting the incumbent firm, the former monopolist, to a variety of constraints from which entrants were exempted—constraints designed to shield the entrants from the consequences of vigorous competition.[19]

The entrants have, of course, seized upon the resulting opportunity to co-opt the regulator into a partnership to impede the incumbent's ability to compete. Lawsuits have been filed, complaints have been made to the regulator, and every other legal avenue has been employed either to adopt rules to handicap the incumbent directly or to delay its competitive responses to the entrant's business strategies.

---

18. *See* MICHAEL K. KELLOGG, JOHN THORNE & PETER W. HUBER, FEDERAL TELE-COMMUNICATIONS LAW 1, 61–62 (Little, Brown & Co. 1992).

19. One example is the FCC's former policy of "permissive detariffing," by which the agency declined to enforce the rate-filing requirements in 47 U.S.C. § 203 against carriers it deemed to be "nondominant." Only AT&T was deemed to be "dominant" and thus obliged to make full tariff filings. This policy was held to violate the Communications Act in American Tel. & Tel. Co. *v.* FCC, 978 F.2d 727 (D.C. Cir. 1992). For a concise discussion of the development of this policy, see DANIEL L BRENNER, LAW AND REGULATION OF COMMON CARRIERS IN THE COMMUNICATIONS INDUSTRY 83–102 (Westview Press 1992). The FCC revived this policy in 1993, claiming its new version to be lawful under the Communications Act. *See* Tariff Filing Requirements for Nondominant Common Carriers, Mem. Op. & Ord., CC Dkt. No. 93-36 (released Aug. 18, 1993).

The preceding description is not intended to blame anyone. The scenario is less a melodrama populated by villains and archangels than a Greek drama in which every actor plays the part assigned by fate. The incumbent naturally has no love for entry, and it seeks to avert actions that would provide a competitive advantage to the entrant. The regulator, recognizing that failure by any firm under its jurisdiction will redound to its discredit, is driven to favor the enterprise that it deems the weaker. The weakling usually is the entrant, whose relative lack of experience and typically smaller size stimulate the regulator's protective instincts. And the entrant—having been provided the opportunity to compete not exclusively by achieving efficient operation or offering superior products (if it can do so), but also by using the legal system to handicap its rivals—can be relied upon to resort to the regulator's protection.

All too often, the result is a bizarre set of rules designed to protect the entrant at the incumbent's expense. In the long run, however, this scenario is usually adopted at the expense of the public. Two illustrations are the unequal treatment of AT&T and its rivals in the interexchange market,[20] and the measures adopted by Oftel, the British regulatory agency, to protect Mercury against BT (British Telecom).[21] These rules protect competitors at the expense of competition. The incumbent is forced to charge prices higher than it would in a truly competitive market, in order to make it easier for the entrant to lure its customers away. The incumbent must also supply facilities and services to the entrant at prices below the competitive-market level—a forced subsidy. The incentives for efficiency are obviously undermined, and consumer choices are distorted by arbitrary prices. In some cases, regulatory actions have effectively confined the entrant and the incumbent to different markets—for example, excluding the incumbent from the supply of telecommunications services to large business firms, and excluding the entrant from the residential arena. Of course, that policy is the antithesis of vigorous competition. It is tantamount to creating a governmentally imposed cartel. The dangers of such an arrangement

---

20. *See* note 19 *supra*.

21. *See* Eli Noam, Telecommunications in Europe 110–13 (Oxford Univ. Press 1992); John Vickers & George Yarrow, Privatization: An Economic Analysis 229–30, 238–39 (MIT Press 1988).

to the general welfare are exacerbated by the regulator's belief that it contributes to competitiveness and benefits the public, because the presence of two firms in a market is deemed better than one, no matter what it takes to retain them there.

Yet sometimes concerns about the initial difficulties of entry into some lines of activity may well be valid. To the extent that capital markets are imperfect, the new small entrant may indeed be placed at a disadvantage.[22] A further handicap can well be present if the minimum efficient scale for a firm—that is, the volume of output and the value of sunk investment necessary to enable it to compete effectively[23]—is large. It then can conceivably benefit society to make the entrant's task easier.

The entrant should be assisted if entry is impeded by imperfections of the capital markets or entry barriers that impose special costs upon the new enterprise. But the task then is to devise means to encourage entry without undermining the competitive process by means such as the imposition of artificial prices, output quotas, or interfirm cross-subsidies. If the problem is unavailability of funds, for example, it may be appropriate to provide some form of insurance to the new firm on its borrowings—that is, governmental loan guarantees. But if the benefits expected from entry will accrue to the general public, it is inappropriate to extract the cost of the insurance from particular firms or

---

22. We follow the late Professor George Stigler's definition of an entry barrier as an arrangement that imposes a cost upon an entrant from which an incumbent is immune. GEORGE J. STIGLER, THE ORGANIZATION OF INDUSTRY 67 (Richard D. Irwin, Inc. 1968). Thus, capital market imperfections are not, in themselves, entry barriers. *See* GEORGE J. STIGLER, THE THEORY OF PRICE 208 (Macmillan Publishing Co., 4th ed. 1987); George J. Stigler, *Imperfections in the Capital Markets*, 75 J. POL. ECON. 287 (1967). Where large sunk investments are required, however, the second firm to enter a market is likely to face higher funding costs than its predecessor's because the entrant faces an added risk of strategic entry countermeasures by the incumbent. This is not an imperfection in the capital market, but represents its accurate pricing of risk. Moreover, capital market imperfections that are costly to every firm in the industry can reduce the number of firms that can operate profitably in the arena, and they can in that sense inhibit entry, even though they do not favor one firm over another, or protect the incumbent from market pressures when it seeks to adopt prices that exceed competitive levels. Consequences like this last, of course, are what make Stigler's definition of an entry barrier so useful.

23. *See, e.g.*, DENNIS W. CARLTON & JEFFREY M. PERLOFF, MODERN INDUSTRIAL ORGANIZATION 47–48 (Scott, Foresman/Little, Brown Higher Education 1990).

groups of telecommunications customers. Above all, it is inappropriate to distort prices, or to destroy or suspend effective competition by the incumbent, in order to encourage the entrant—even where some incentive to the entrant is justifiable in terms of the public interest. The issue has arisen in several countries where the formerly nationalized telecommunications monopoly has been privatized.[24] The hope that its behavior will then be appropriately circumscribed by competitive forces depends on the feasibility of entry. In these circumstances, one can understand concerns about what forms of assistance to the entrant are appropriate. More difficult to comprehend are the regulatory impediments to effective competition by the privatized firm that have sometimes been employed to ease matters for the entrant. Such measures undermine competition for the sake of the competitor.

A Possibly Pareto-Superior Alternative to Line-of-Business Restrictions: The Bifurcation Rule

The MFJ originally prohibited the seven regional Bell operating companies from offering information services, and it continues to prohibit the RBOCs from either transmitting messages across the boundaries separating the LATAs or from manufacturing telecommunications equipment.[25] These line-of-business restrictions are based on concerns about cross-subsidy and predatory pricing. But perhaps the goals of this quarantine approach can be attained by less restrictive means that promise to improve social welfare in other respects.[26] This question is especially timely, given the petition filed by five RBOCs in

24. *See* VICKERS & YARROW, *supra* note 21, at 238.

25. In 1993, the United States Court of Appeals for the District of Columbia Circuit affirmed the lifting of the restrictions preventing the RBOCs from offering information services to their customers. United States *v.* Western Elec. Co., 993 F.2d 1572 (D.C. Cir. 1993). That result, however, can be modified or reversed by legislation. In 1992, the House Judiciary Committee approved a bill that would have reaffirmed and expanded by statute all the MFJ's line-of-business restrictions. H.R. 5096, 102d Cong., 2d Sess. (1992). *See also* H.R. REP. NO. 850, 102d Cong., 2d Sess. (1992).

26. A more detailed version of the following discussion appears in J. Gregory Sidak, *Telecommunications in Jericho*, 80 CALIF. L. REV. (forthcoming Oct. 1993).

July 1993 requesting the FCC to promulgate rules governing their entry into the interLATA market.[27]

The cross-subsidy or predation scenario at issue needs to be spelled out briefly in order to clarify the policy proposal to be offered presently. The problem about which one is concerned is the possibility that a LEC, having acquired control of an unregulated firm that manufactures telecommunications equipment, will be tempted to make expenditures at the LEC's own expense, expenditures whose benefits go to its manufacturing affiliate. If the regulator can be persuaded that this expenditure is a legitimate cost of the LEC's activity, he can be expected to permit the LEC to increase its revenues through exercise of its market power by an amount sufficient to cover that cost. In that way, the competitive position of the LEC's affiliate can be improved at the expense of the LEC's customers.

Predation Versus Forgone Product Innovation. The MFJ's line-of-business restrictions derive from the risk to consumers of cross-subsidization and predation, yet they ignore the forgone consumers' surplus from services that the RBOCs would or might offer but for the restrictions.[28] It is possible, however, that the expectable welfare loss from any cross-subsidization and predation that may arise in the wake of the RBOCs' entry into competitive markets is less than the corresponding loss from denial or postponement of consumers' access to new communications services that the RBOCs, because of economies of scope in information or research, may be able to introduce sooner than other firms can. Several RBOCs believe, for example, that "telemedicine" can significantly reduce some health care costs for the public; but the introduction of such services is constrained, they argue, by the MFJ's prohibition against RBOC transport of long-distance traffic across LATA boundaries. It is difficult to assess such a claim *ex ante.* From the limited anecdotal evidence, however, we cannot

---

27. Petition of Bell Atlantic, BellSouth Corp., NYNEX Corp., Pacific Telesis Group, and Southwestern Bell Corp. for Rulemaking to Determine the Terms and Conditions Under Which Tier 1 LECs Should Be Permitted to Provide InterLATA Telecommunications Services (filed before the FCC July 15, 1993).

28. As we will observe presently, a flexible regulatory profit ceiling, such as is permitted by a price-cap regime of the sort described in Chapter 6, is by itself a major step toward elimination of any special incentive for a *regulated* firm to engage in cross-subsidy or predation.

conclude that this kind of forgone consumer surplus is negligible. After the RBOCs were permitted to offer voice mail as an information service in 1988, for example, "the voice mail equipment market grew threefold and prices declined dramatically."[29]

To maximize social welfare, government policy on entry in telecommunications should aim to minimize the *sum* of welfare losses from predation and from new products forgone, rather than minimizing only the former without regard for the magnitude of the latter. The policy imperative should be to minimize the combined damage attributable to monopoly and regulation, while awaiting the advent of effectively competitive or contestable markets in local telephony. The same argument applies to a LEC's entry into video programming in the geographic area where it provides telephone service—in contrast to mere common carriage of such programming in its service area, which is not forbidden by regulation or statute. For ease of exposition, our discussion deals only with line-of-business restrictions in terms of the MFJ's current entry constraints on the RBOCs.

Bifurcating Ownership and Control in the Unregulated Affiliate. Is there some preferable arrangement, intermediate between regulation and its complete elimination, that can deal effectively with the tradeoff between delayed innovation and the risk of predation? We will suggest one such possibility. Even if the risk of cross-subsidy and predation by the RBOCs is deemed too high to justify vacating of the MFJ, there may be an efficacious alternative that is less restrictive than total prohibition of RBOC entry into particular unregulated markets. We will call this alternative the *bifurcation rule*.

The RBOCs seek to enter adjacent markets themselves, rather than sharing, through confidential technology-licensing agreements, proprietary information with separate firms that are not local exchange carriers. The RBOCs explain their preference for direct market entry by arguing that control by their management is necessary to exploit fully the RBOC's telecommunications knowledge. The bifurcation rule permits an RBOC to enter a currently-prohibited market, but only through a separate, publicly traded corporation having two classes of stock—one with voting rights but with a negligible claim to the affiliat-

29. Kellogg, Thorne & Huber, *supra* note 18, at 396.

ed corporation's residual net cash flows, the other with negligible (or no) voting rights but with a claim to virtually all the affiliate's residual net cash flows. While this capital structure permits the RBOC to exercise management control over the unregulated affiliate, it still undermines the RBOC's ability to benefit from cross-subsidization and predation. Under the proposal, regulators can cap the RBOC's ownership of the affiliate's cash flows at any desired percentage figure, including one below 51 percent.[30]

This arrangement inhibits cross-subsidy by reducing its reward to the controlling parent company. To see how this works, suppose that the unregulated firm tries to misattribute costs to the rate-regulated activities of its parent RBOC so as to raise the profit permitted to the regulated parent, using the gain to underprice efficient rivals in the unregulated market.[31] Because of the ownership cap on cash flows, however, the RBOC would receive only some fraction of the monopoly profit that the unregulated firm can hope to earn eventually as a result of its enhanced competitive position made possible by the cross-subsidy. Obviously, if that fraction were less than 50 percent, most of the monopoly profits would enrich not the RBOC but the other holders of the reduced-voting (or nonvoting) stock—who could not be affiliated with the RBOC under the bifurcation rule. Moreover, there is some probability that the improper allocation of cost to the RBOC will be detected and disallowed by regulators. If that happened, the RBOC's unregulated affiliate could then underprice efficient competitors only by sacrificing profit. Its likelihood of attaining monopoly power would then be no greater than it is for any unregulated firm seeking to monopolize any unregulated market through predatory pricing.

---

30. Although the efficiency justification for separation of ownership from control in the corporation is well understood—*see* FRANK H. EASTERBROOK & DANIEL R. FISCHEL, THE ECONOMIC STRUCTURE OF CORPORATE LAW 109–44 (Harvard Univ. Press 1991); Eugene F. Fama & Michael C. Jensen, *Separation of Ownership and Control*, 26 J. LAW & ECON. 301 (1983)—to our knowledge no literature examines how that separation can be used to improve regulatory regimes for natural monopolies.

31. This cross-subsidy problem is most likely to arise under a fixed regulatory profit ceiling—that is, rate-base rate-of-return regulation. Under the price-cap form of regulation advocated in this monograph, the scenario under discussion is far less likely to arise because the LEC faces no fixed profit ceiling, which it may only be able to raise through misattribution of costs actually incurred on behalf of an unregulated affiliate.

The more confidence we have that regulators will detect cross-subsidization, the higher can be the ceiling on the RBOC's percentage ownership of the residual net cash flows of an unregulated firm competing in a market into which the MFJ currently forbids the RBOC's entry. On the other hand, the more plausible it is that a strategy of cross-subsidy can profit an RBOC entering an unregulated market, the lower must be the ceiling on the RBOC's ownership of the affiliated firm in that market.

Benefits and Costs of the Bifurcation Rule. The bifurcation rule may well prove to be as efficacious as the MFJ's line-of-business restrictions in deterring cross-subsidy and predation—especially if the rule were adopted in conjunction with a flexible profit ceiling for the LEC, under the pricing rules discussed earlier. Yet, unlike the MFJ, the bifurcation rule offers the possibility that significant benefits will accrue to at least some consumers, in the form of superior product innovation, when an RBOC is permitted to enter the MFJ's forbidden markets. Because it permits at least some consumers to be made better off, and protects all consumers from the damaging effects of cross-subsidy, the bifurcation rule appears to be Pareto-superior to the MFJ's line-of-business restrictions. By the same reasoning, the bifurcation rule appears to be Pareto-superior to any analogous line-of-business restriction, such as the cable-telco entry ban.[32]

The bifurcation rule also seems to be better suited than the MFJ to periodic review of whether the regulation is serving its intended purpose or is in need of modification. By requiring that both classes of stock in the unregulated firm be traded publicly on a national exchange, regulators can readily measure the level of the RBOC's current share of ownership of the affiliate's cash flows. The bifurcation rule thus changes the evaluation of an RBOC's entry into an adjacent market from one requiring a discrete yes-no decision to one permitting

---

32. In 1992, the FCC granted a limited exception from the video cross-ownership prohibition, allowing a telephone company to own as much as 5 percent of a video programmer operating within the LEC's region. Telephone Company-Cable Television Cross-Ownership Rules, Sections 63.54–63.58, Second Rep. & Order, Recommendations to Congress, & Second Further Notice of Proposed Rulemaking, CC Dkt. No. 87-266, 7 F.C.C. Rcd. 5781, 5801-02 ¶ 36 (1992). This ruling, however, does not bifurcate ownership and control, nor is it designed—as is the bifurcation rule—to adjust automatically to the increasing competitiveness or contestability of the market for local exchange.

continuity in the decision. Moreover, that decision can be revised with little administrative burden. As regulators observe economic performance in the unregulated market, they may decide to raise the RBOC's ownership ceiling, or to reduce it.

If cross-subsidy were to become a serious threat, divestiture of the RBOC's stake in the unregulated firm could be carried out swiftly by a court order requiring the RBOC to sell its stock. The fact that a court-ordered divestiture could be carried out so expeditiously after a finding of anticompetitive behavior would yield the incidental benefit of sharpening the RBOC's incentive for competitive behavior in the unregulated market.

It should be acknowledged that the bifurcation rule apparently does have some efficiency costs. First, because it offers the RBOC only a limited percentage of any gains generated by its innovations through its affiliate, the incentive for investment and research by the RBOC will clearly be reduced. Second, the rule can constitute an impediment to incentive compensation plans because such a program, if it is based on the offer of stock options to the managers of the affiliate, would in effect give control of the dividends associated with those shares indirectly to the RBOC through its control of the affiliate. Third, and probably most important, there is the danger that any attempt to erect an effective wall between the RBOC and its affiliate will entail some loss, perhaps even substantial, of economies of scope. This must constitute an inefficiency and an artificially imposed cost increase. Certainly, this last cost was experienced when the FCC decreed that AT&T could offer computer-related "enhanced" services only through a separate subsidiary.[33] The bifurcation rule, with its market-based rules and its built-in flexibility, is very different from this former FCC policy, but they can have similar implications for economies of scope. Still, on balance, the bifurcation rule offers sufficient promise to merit its serious consideration.

---

33. Amendment of § 64.702 of the Commission's Rules & Regulations, Second Computer Inquiry (*Computer II*), 77 F.C.C.2d 384, *modified on recon.*, 84 F.C.C.2d 50 (1980), *further modified on recon.*, 88 F.C.C.2d 512 (1981), *aff'd sub nom.* Computer & Comm. Indus. Ass'n v. FCC, 693 F.2d 198 (D.C. Cir. 1982), *cert. denied*, 461 U.S. 938 (1983). For a discussion of this proceeding and the subsequent *Computer III* proceeding reversing it, see KELLOGG, THORNE & HUBER, *supra* note 18, at 537–68.

Conclusion

As we indicated in Chapter 2, competitive entry now threatens to become effective in provision of the local loop and access to that loop. The threat assumes at least three forms. The most conjectural source of prospective competition at present is wireless access through cellular radio technology. The most obvious is the rival specialized telecommunications carrier, which serves larger customer traffic within the local exchange by more or less traditional means brought up to date by current technology. Previously such entry had generally been thought to offer no likelihood of profitable operation. Yet the evolution of technology is making this prospect a reality elsewhere. If this form of competition can be introduced successfully in New Zealand, surely it will soon be feasible in the United States. Once such entry is permitted in a state having a relatively flexible public utilities commission and proves itself successful, applications for entry elsewhere can be expected to proliferate.

But perhaps the most immediate threat to monopoly in the local loop has come from the suppliers of cable television services who, having already wired millions of American households, can exploit the economies of scope offered by simultaneously providing both telecommunications and television transmission services. Predictably, the cable companies would like permission to enter local telephony in the same markets in which they provide cable service. But their plea, if granted, sets a dangerous political precedent for the cable companies. The LECs can play the opposite game, and plead for corresponding regulatory relief permitting them to become providers of video programming in their areas of local exchange service.

Great benefit can redound to the public interest from adoption of regulatory rules for local telephony that adjust automatically as the market structure evolves from natural monopoly toward something closer to perfect competition or perfect contestability. Like the efficient component-pricing rule for inputs sold by the LEC to its competitors, and like the average-incremental-cost price floor and stand-alone-cost ceiling for services that can be produced only by a naturally monopolistic local exchange carrier, the rules proposed or explored in this chapter to promote entry have built-in adaptability. Like those pricing rules, these rules for market entry will become superfluous, but innocuous, if and when the market for local exchange has become highly competitive or contestable.

9

Conclusion: Toward a
Revised Regulatory System

THIS CHAPTER OFFERS a few thoughts on the relation of the regulatory principles described here to an operational and effective program in practice, including a few remarks suggesting that the political obstacles to such a transition are hardly insurmountable, as recent experience demonstrates. But first, a few more words should be said about means to reduce any burdens entailed in carrying out the regulatory principles that have been described here.

We have already discussed the burdens upon the regulated firm, its competitors, and the regulators involved in calculating average-incremental cost, marginal cost, and stand-alone cost. A number of legitimate approximating shortcuts can ease the task. We have provided several theorems on the equivalence of incremental costs and stand-alone costs, and we have described the full set of incremental-cost calculations meeting all the combinatorial requirements, and the full set of stand-alone cost calculations. We have seen why it is unnecessary to calculate both the price floor and the price ceiling. We have briefly described the basket-of-services approach to price-cap regulation—in which sets of related services are grouped together, and the price cap is applied only to the average price of the services in the basket, rather than to the individual prices, service by service.

Grouping Basic Network Functions as a Means to Lighten the Burden of Regulation

A similar grouping of the basic network functions (BNFs) described in Chapter 8 can facilitate the regulation of pricing by the suppliers of local telephone services. The BNFs can be grouped according to similarities in competitive circumstances, relationships in production, and similarities in the groups of customers that purchase them. It is important that BNFs sharing common equipment be grouped together, because of problems of cross-subsidy and the difficulties besetting coverage of common costs. Then it can more easily be decided whether a particular group of BNFs can safely be deregulated or at least partially deregulated, whether regulation should soon should be phased out, or whether the group should be subjected to the full mechanism of regulation described here. Aggregation into baskets of basic network functions not only should facilitate calculation and testing, but also should simplify the task of regulatory oversight.

The Danger of Adopting Only Part of the Program

Socially optimal regulation of local telephony is composed of a number of parts, and those parts can serve their purpose *only* if they are adopted and carried out together. Execution of only a few of the optimality rules does not guarantee even an improvement in economic efficiency because of the proposition in economics called the theorem of the second best.[1] The theorem asserts that if, for example, five requirements must be satisfied to achieve economic efficiency, then a program that satisfies four but violates the fifth may make things worse than if none of the five conditions had been met.

That admonition is warranted here. We have seen, for example, that the efficient component-pricing rule is a requirement of economic efficiency. But if this rule is enforced by legislation or regulatory practice without simultaneously adopting the appropriate ceiling for

---

1. *See* Richard G. Lipsey & Kevin Lancaster, *The General Theory of Second Best*, 24 REV. ECON. STUD. 11 (1956). *See also* Arnold C. Harberger, *Three Postulates for Applied Welfare Analysis*, 9 J. ECON. LIT. 785 (1971).

prices, the result may prove unattractive. The regulated firm not only will be permitted to earn monopoly profits from final-product consumers because of the lack of a proper price cap, but also will be permitted by the pricing rule to extract similar monopoly profits, in the form of opportunity costs, from competing enterprises to which the regulated firm sells inputs such as access.

The moral is clear. The legislature or regulatory agency that seeks to protect the public interest cannot adopt only a highly truncated part of the program described here. Partial adoption may be politically expedient, but a course that undertakes to institute only a subset of the requirements prescribed by the competitive-market model for regulation cannot be expected to improve matters, much less to constitute a maximal contribution to the public welfare.

The Coherence of the Logic of the Regulatory Structure

We have covered considerable terrain in this monograph. It has examined the logic of the price ceilings that can appropriately protect consumers of local telephone services from exploitation through exercise of monopoly power. It has analyzed the price floors that prevent cross-subsidy, predatory pricing, and pricing whose only rationale is to weaken competition. It has described the rules required for economic efficiency governing the pricing of inputs sold to rivals of the input supplier in the marketing of final products. It has shown how those rules comport with the competitive-market model for regulation, and how they promote economic efficiency. Finally, it has examined the circumstances in which deregulation is the course that most effectively promotes the public interest; the same analysis has been used to suggest the desirability of removing regulatory barriers inhibiting the entry of suppliers of local telephone service and cable television carriers (and others) into one another's territories.

One feature pervading this monograph is the logical coherence of the entire regulatory structure described. The analysis is a logical consequence of the competitive-market model—that is, the model of perfect contestability as a defensible guide for regulation of local telephone services. Once that premise is embraced, all the rest follows.

None of it is *ad hoc* or ambiguous—and this alone would constitute an improvement over the approaches of earlier regulation that arose from tradition and from the happenstances of evolving practice, having no discernible basis in the logic of promotion of economic welfare.

Much of the discussion has stressed the properties of static economic efficiency of the regulatory rules proposed. But the flexible earnings permitted under the price-cap approach are designed to supply the incentives required to elicit investment in innovation and enhanced productivity. Thus the program also addresses itself to the encouragement of improved intertemporal performance. In sum, the constrained-market pricing approach to regulation is intended to be a workable program that seeks to prevent interference with the achievement of either static efficiency or growth performance.

One of the most powerful arguments supporting the regulatory approach described here is that, despite all the prospective sources for competition in local telephony, it is impossible either to foretell the degree to which such competition will take hold or to predict the sectors of local telecommunications activity where it will succeed and those where it will not. Our proposal seeks to obviate the risks detailed in dependence upon unreliable forecasts, instead allowing the market to decide the issue. If entry is permitted subject to the safeguards described here, the risks to the public interest will be minimized. In those activities where vigorous competition materializes, the regulations will soon become redundant and should be allowed to wither away. Where healthy competition does not emerge, the rules will protect the public interest from the exercise of market power by the local telephone companies. Whichever scenario unfolds, either the forces of competition or the regulatory rules should stimulate efficiency and productivity growth.

The Political Economy of Adoption

There remain many difficult, practical problems that will have to be dealt with before such a program can be instituted. Is the FCC likely to have the desire and the political independence to undertake it? Will the intervention of Congress be required and, if so, how can Congress be induced to do so? What cooperation will be required and expected from state public utility commissions? Will regulatory bodies voluntarily relinquish their authority as the power of competition grows?

Recent developments invite a degree of optimism. Promising steps, in this industry and others, have been taken all along the line—beginning with the Civil Aeronautics Board's self-imposed demise, and continuing with the adoption of constrained-market pricing by the Interstate Commerce Commission, price caps by the FCC, and corresponding steps by various state regulatory agencies.

But further consideration of such essentially political issues is beyond our competence, and so the discussion here must end with these matters left for those better suited to the task.

Glossary

Access service: Service that enables an individual user (either an individual subscriber or an interexchange carrier) to connect to the switching system of a local exchange carrier.

Alternative access provider (ALT): A carrier that competes with the local exchange carrier by offering high-capacity dedicated lines for business customers and interexchange carriers—and, potentially, for smaller users, through switched services. Also called a competitive access provider (CAP).

Basic network functions (BNFs): Individual functions performed by the local exchange carrier that involve the use of loops, switches, signaling, and transport.

Bypass: The circumvention of a telecommunications facility by means of a lower-cost alternative, such as satellite, microwave, or private line.

Cable telephony: Use of a cable television distribution system to transmit and switch voice and data in a manner functionally equivalent to the public switched telephone network.

Cellular telephony: A wireless telecommunications system, used extensively for mobile communications, that divides a geographic region into cells, uses a low-power transmitter within each cell, and reuses transmission frequencies in cells that are not contiguous.

Competitive access provider (CAP): *See* Alternative access provider.

Digital compression: A technique that enables a given message, such as a television picture, to be converted from an analog signal to a digitized code of data that occupies a smaller amount of transmission capacity than the original analog signal. This technique can effectively increase the amount of usable spectrum currently allocated and expand the number of available channels on cable television systems.

Enhanced services: Telephone services that alter the format or content of information transmitted by the subscriber.

Fiber-optic network: A network made of glass or plastic cables that employs pulses of light to transport large quantities of information.

Full-service network: A vertically integrated telecommunications network for the transmission, switching, and storage of voice messages, data, and video images for use by business, residential, and mobile customers. Such networks prospectively may combine different forms of technology, such as wireless access, fiber-optic transmission, cable television networks, and conventional local telephone networks.

Information services: Telephone services requiring the manipulation of information (such as on-line data retrieval), as opposed to mere transport of such information. The regional Bell operating companies originally were prohibited under the Modification of Final Judgment from offering such services.

Interconnection: The linkage of one telecommunications network to another, such as the linkage of an interexchange carrier to a local exchange carrier in order to complete a long-distance call.

Interexchange carrier (IXC): A telecommunication carrier, such as AT&T or MCI, that is authorized to provide "long-distance" service between local access and transport areas.

Local access and transport area (LATA): Following the AT&T divestiture, a local market for exchange services provided by a Bell operating company; pursuant to the Modification of Final Judgment, Bell operating companies may not transport calls across LATA boundaries, but rather must switch them to interexchange carriers.

Local area network (LAN): A high-speed data communications network in which all segments of the transmission medium are within the users' premises.

Local exchange carrier (LEC): A provider of local transport and exchange service—the local telephone company.

Metropolitan area network (MAN): A private communications network that crosses public rights-of-way and is located within an area no more than 50 kilometers in diameter.

Modification of Final Judgment (MFJ): The consent decree that effected the divestiture of AT&T and imposed various line-of-business restrictions on the regional Bell operating companies.

Multiple system operator (MSO): A cable television operator, such as Time Warner Inc. or Tele-Communications, Inc. (TCI), that provides service through more than one regional cable television system.

Personal communications services (PCS): Any one of many prospective services or systems, such as pocket telephones, that will provide direct wireless access by means of low-power cells analogous to those used in cellular telephony. Also called personal communications networks (PCN).

Private branch exchange (PBX): A switching system located on the customer's premises that connects internal calls and provides access to outside telecommunications networks.

Regional Bell operating company (RBOC): One of seven regional companies that assumed ownership, following the AT&T divestiture, of the local exchange activities of the former Bell System. They are Ameritech, Bell Atlantic, BellSouth, NYNEX, Pacific Telesis, Southwestern Bell, and U S West.

Wide-area network (WAN): A private telecommunications network that provides services beyond the distance limitations of metropolitan area networks—for example, linking distant offices of a single company.

References

American Telephone & Telegraph Company, 1992 *Annual Report* (1993).

Andrews, Edmund L., "The Local Call Goes up for Grabs," *New York Times*, Dec. 29, 1991, § 3 (Business), at 1.

Areeda, Phillip, and Donald F. Turner, "Predatory Pricing and Related Practices Under Section 2 of the Sherman Act," 88 *Harvard Law Review* 637 (1975).

Arrow, Kenneth J., "An Extension of the Basic Theorems of Classical Welfare Economics," in *Proceedings of the Second Berkeley Symposium on Mathematical Statistics and Probability* (Jerzy Neyman ed., University of California Press 1951).

Averch, Harvey, and Leland L. Johnson, "Behavior of the Firm under Regulatory Constraint," 52 *American Economic Review* 1053 (1962).

Barnett, William P., and Glenn R. Carroll, "How Institutional Constraints Affected the Organization of Early U.S. Telephony," 9 *Journal of Law, Economics & Organization* 98 (1993).

Baumol, William J., "Reasonable Rules for Rate Regulation, Plausible Policies for an Imperfect World," in Almarin Philips and Oliver E.

Williamson, *Prices: Issues in Theory, Practice and Public Policy* (University of Pennsylvania Press 1968).

Baumol, William J., "Productivity Incentive Clauses and Rate Adjustment for Inflation," *Public Utilities Fortnightly,* vol. 110., no. 2 (July 22, 1982).

Baumol, William J., *Superfairness: Applications and Theory* (MIT Press 1986).

Baumol, William J., Elizabeth E. Bailey, and Robert D. Willig, "Weak Invisible Hand Theorems on the Sustainability of Multiproduct Natural Monopoly," 67 *American Economic Review* 350 (1977).

Baumol, William J., and David F. Bradford, "Optimal Departures From Marginal Cost Pricing," 60 *American Economic Review* 265 (1970).

Baumol, William J., Michael F. Koehn, and Robert D. Willig, "How Arbitrary Is 'Arbitrary'?—or, Toward the Deserved Demise of Full Cost Allocation," *Public Utilities Fortnightly*, vol. 120, no. 5, (September 3, 1987).

Baumol, William J., and Wallace E. Oates, *The Theory of Environmental Policy* (Cambridge University Press 2d ed. 1988).

Baumol, William J., John C. Panzar, and Robert D. Willig, *Contestable Markets and the Theory of Industry Structure* (Harcourt Brace Jovanovich rev. ed. 1988).

Bork, Robert H., *The Antitrust Paradox: A Policy at War with Itself* (Free Press 1978).

Bork, Robert H., *The Antitrust Paradox: A Policy at War with Itself* (Free Press rev. ed. 1993).

Braeutigam, Ronald R., and John C. Panzar, "Effects of the Change from Rate of Return to Price Cap Regulation," 83 *American Economic Review Papers and Proceedings* 191 (1993).

Brenner, Daniel L., *Law and Regulation of Common Carriers in the Communications Industry* (Westview Press 1992).

Breyer, Stephen G., *Regulation and Its Reform* (Harvard University Press 1982).

Breyer, Stephen G., "Antitrust, Deregulation, and the Newly Liberated Marketplace," 75 *California Law Review* 1005 (1987).

Brozen, Yale, *Concentration, Mergers, and Public Policy* (Macmillan Publishing Co. 1982).

"Cable-Phone Link Is Promising Gamble: Time Warner Sees Synergy in Partnership," *Wall Street Journal,* May 18, 1993, at B1.

Calhoun, George C., *Wireless Access and the Local Telephone Network* (Artech House, Inc. 1992).

Carlton, Dennis W., and Jeffrey M. Perloff, *Modern Industrial Organization* (Scott, Foresman/Little, Brown Higher Education 1990).

Carnevale, Mary Lu, "AT&T-McCaw Link Stuns Baby Bells," *Wall Street Journal*, Nov. 6, 1992, at B1.

Carnevale, Mary Lu, "Pacific Telesis Plan to Split Up Poses Challenge," *Wall Street Journal*, Dec. 12, 1992, at A3.

"Clear and Telecom NZ Both Claim Victory in Local Access Case," *Exchange*, vol. 5, no. 1 (Jan. 15, 1993).

"Clear Takes Telecom NZ Back to Court," *Exchange*, vol. 5, no. 1 (Feb. 12, 1993).

Crandall, Robert W., *After the Breakup: U.S. Telecommunications in a More Competitive Era* (Brookings Institution 1991).

Crandall, Robert W., "Regulating Communications: Creating Monopoly While 'Protecting' Us From It," *Brookings Review*, vol. 10, no. 3, (Summer 1992).

Debreu, Gerard, "The Coefficient of Resource Utilization," 19 *Econometrica* 273 (1951).

Debreu, Gerard, *Theory of Value: An Axiomatic Analysis of Economic Equilibrium* (Yale University Press 1959).

Diamond, Peter A., and John A. Mirrlees, "Optimal Taxation and Public Production, II: Tax Rules," 61 *American Economic Review* 261 (1971).

Easterbrook, Frank H., "Predatory Strategies and Counterstrategies," 48 *University of Chicago Law Review* 263 (1981).

Easterbrook, Frank H., and Daniel R. Fischel, *The Economic Structure of Corporate Law* (Harvard University Press 1991).

Economic Report of the President, 1988.

Fama, Eugene F., and Michael C. Jensen, "Separation of Ownership and Control," 26 *Journal of Law and Economics* 301 (1983).

Farmer, James, "Transition from Protected Monopoly to Competition: The New Zealand Experiment," 1 *Competition and Consumer Law Journal* 1 (1993).

Faulhaber, Gerald R., "Cross-Subsidization: Pricing in Public Enterprise," 65 *American Economic Review* 966 (1975).

Faulhaber, Gerald R., and Stephen B. Levinson, "Subsidy-Free Prices and Anonymous Equity," 71 *American Economic Review* 1083 (1981).

Hall, Terry, "From Monopoly to Competitor—New Zealand/Pacific Rim," *Financial Times*, Oct. 7, 1991, § III (World Communications), at 30.

Harberger, Arnold C., "Three Postulates for Applied Welfare Analysis," 9 *Journal of Economic Literature* 785 (1971).

Hazlett, Thomas W., "Private Monopoly and the Public Interest: An Economic Analysis of the Cable Television Franchise," 134 *University of Pennsylvania Law Review* 1335 (1986).

Hazlett, Thomas W., "Duopolistic Competition in CATV: Implications for Public Policy," 7 *Yale Journal of Regulation* 65 (1990).

Hazlett, Thomas W., "The Demand to Regulate Franchise Monopoly: Evidence from CATV Rate Deregulation in California," 29 *Economic Inquiry* 275 (1991).

Huber, Peter W., Michael K. Kellogg, and John Thorne, *The Geodesic Network II: 1993 Report on Competition in the Telephone Industry* (The Geodesic Co. 1992).

Kahn, Alfred E., *The Economics of Regulation: Principles and Institutions* (MIT Press rev. ed. 1988).

Kaserman, David L., John W. Mayo, Larry Blank, and Simran Kahai, "Open Entry and Local Telephone Rates: The Economics of Intra-LATA Toll Competition," 6 *Journal of Regulatory Economics* (forthcoming 1994).

Keller, John J., "Cellular Move Underscores AT&T's Transformation," *Wall Street Journal*, Nov. 6, 1992, at B1.

Keller, John J., "AT&T Agrees to Buy McCaw Cellular in Stock Swap Valued at $12.6 Billion," *Wall Street Journal,* August 17, 1993, at A3.

Kellogg, Michael K., John Thorne, and Peter W. Huber, *Federal Telecommunications Law* (Little, Brown & Co. 1992).

Klevorick, Alvin K., "The Current State of the Law and Economics of Predatory Pricing," 83 *American Economic Review Papers and Proceedings* 162 (1993).

Kreps, David M., *A Course in Microeconomic Theory* (Princeton University Press 1990).

Laffont, Jean-Jacques, and Jean Tirole, *The Theory of Incentives in Procurement and Regulation* (MIT Press 1993).

Landes, William E., and Richard A. Posner, "Market Power in Antitrust Cases," 94 *Harvard Law Review* 937 (1981).

Landro, Laura, Johnnie L. Roberts, and Randall Smith, "Cable Phone Link Is Promising Gamble: Time Warner Sees Synergy in Partnership," *Wall Street Journal*, May 18, 1993, at B1.

Lenard, Thomas M., Monica F. Bettendorf, and Stephen McGonegal, "Stand-Alone Costs, Ramsey Prices, and Postal Rates," 4 *Journal of Regulatory Economics* 243 (1992).

Lipsey, Richard G., and Kevin Lancaster, "The General Theory of Second Best," 24 *Review of Economic Studies* 11 (1956).

MacAvoy, Paul W., *Industry Regulation and the Performance of the American Economy* (W.W. Norton & Company 1992).

MacAvoy, Paul W., and Kenneth Robinson, "Winning by Losing: The AT&T Settlement and Its Impact on Telecommunications," 1 *Yale Journal on Regulation* 1 (1983).

McCaw Cellular Communications Corporation, 1992 *Annual Report* (1993).

McCaw Cellular Communications Corporation, 1992 *Form 10-K* (1993).

MFS Communications Corporation, *Prospectus for 8,000,000 Shares*, (Apr. 21, 1993).

Mitchell, Bridger M., and Ingo Vogelsang, *Telecommunications Pricing: Theory and Practice* (Cambridge University Press 1991).

Morrison, Steven A., and Clifford Winston, *The Evolution of the Airline Industry* (Brookings Institution forthcoming 1994).

National Association of Regulatory Utility Commissioners, *The Status of Competition in Intrastate Telecommunications* (1992).

The New Palgrave Dictionary of Economics (John Eatwell, Murray Milgate & Peter Newman, eds., Macmillan Press Limited 1987).

Noam, Eli, *Telecommunications in Europe* (Oxford University Press 1992).

Pacific Telesis Group, 1992 *Form 10-K* (1993).

Pecar, Joseph A., Roger J. O'Connor, and David A. Garbin, *The McGraw-Hill Telecommunications Factbook* (McGraw-Hill, Inc. 1993).

Posner, Richard A., *Antitrust Law: An Economic Perspective* (University of Chicago Press 1976).

Ramsey, Frank, "A Contribution to the Theory of Taxation," 37 *Economic Journal* 47 (1927).

Roberts, Johnnie L., and Mary Lu Carnevale, "Time Warner Plans Electronic Superhighway," *Wall Street Journal*, Jan. 27, 1993, at B10.

Robichaux, Mark, and Mary Lu Carnevale, "Southwestern Bell Reaches Pact to Break Into Cable TV," *Wall Street Journal*, Feb. 10, 1993, at B1.

Rohlfs, Jeffrey, Charles Jackson, and Tracy Kelly, *Estimate of the Loss to the United States Caused by the FCC's Delay in Licensing Cellular Telecommunications* (National Economic Research Associates, Inc., Nov. 1991).

Sherman, Roger, *The Regulation of Monopoly* (Cambridge University Press 1989).

Sidak, J. Gregory, "Debunking Predatory Innovation," 83 *Columbia Law Review* 1121 (1983).

Sidak, J. Gregory, "Telecommunications in Jericho," 80 *California Law Review* (forthcoming 1993).

Snoddy, Raymond, "BT Fears Threat of Cable Competitors," *Financial Times*, Oct. 16, 1992, at 9.

Sprint Corporation, 1992 *Annual Report* (1993).

Spulber, Daniel F., *Regulation and Markets* (MIT Press 1989).

Stigler, George J., "Imperfections in the Capital Markets," 75 *Journal of Political Economy* 287 (1967).

Stigler, George J., *The Organization of Industry* (Richard D. Irwin, Inc. 1968).

Stigler, George J., *The Theory of Price* (Macmillan Publishing Co. 4th ed. 1987).

Taylor, Lester D., *Telecommunications Demand* (Kluwer Academic Publishers forthcoming 1993).

Time Warner, Inc., 1992 *Form 10-K* (1993).

Tirole, Jean, *The Theory of Industrial Organization* (MIT Press 1988).

Train, Kenneth E., *Optimal Regulation: The Economic Theory of Natural Monopoly* (MIT Press 1991).

Tye, William B., *The Theory of Contestable Markets: Applications to Regulatory and Antitrust Problems in the Rail Industry* (Greenwood Press 1990).

Varian, Hal R., *Microeconomic Analysis* (W.W. Norton & Co. 3d ed. 1992).

Vickers, John, and George Yarrow, *Privatization: An Economic Analysis* (MIT Press 1988).

Willig, Robert D., "Consumer Equity and Local Measured Service," in *Perspectives on Local Measured Service* (J.A. Baude *et al.* eds., Telecommunications Industry Workshop, Kansas City 1979).

Case and Regulatory Proceeding Index

Name Index

Subject Index

A NOTE ON THE BOOK

This book was edited by
Cheryl Weissman
of the staff of the AEI Press.
Data Reproductions Corporation,
of Rochester Hills, Michigan,
printed and bound the book,
using permanent acid-free paper.